Cooking School
INDIAN

Cooking School

INDIAN

Bring the flavours of India to life in your own kitchen!

LOVE FOOD™

This edition published in 2011
LOVE FOOD is an imprint of Parragon Books Ltd

Parragon
Queen Street House
4 Queen Street
Bath BA1 1HE, UK

www.parragon.com

ISBN: 978-1-4454-7026-9

Printed in China

Internal design by Pink Creative

Notes for the Reader

This book uses both metric and imperial measurements. Follow the same units of measurement throughout; do not mix metric and imperial. All spoon measurements are level: teaspoons are assumed to be 5 ml, and tablespoons are assumed to be 15 ml. Unless otherwise stated, milk is assumed to be full fat, eggs and individual vegetables are medium, and pepper is freshly ground black pepper.

The times given are an approximate guide only. Preparation times differ according to the techniques used by different people and the cooking times may also vary from those given. Optional ingredients, variations or serving suggestions have not been included in the calculations.

Recipes using raw or very lightly cooked eggs should be avoided by infants, the elderly, pregnant women, convalescents and anyone suffering from an illness. Pregnant and breastfeeding women are advised to avoid eating peanuts and peanut products. Sufferers from nut allergies should be aware that some of the ready-made ingredients used in the recipes in this book may contain nuts. Always check the packaging before use.

Contents

Introduction

In India food is taken very seriously. It is eaten with great appreciation and enjoyment – not just to fill the stomach, but also to fine-tune the body both spiritually and physically according to the ancient system of ayurvedic medicine. Indian cooks who maintain this long-held tradition carefully combine different seasonings and ingredients, adjusting them according to the health and temperament of family members, and also taking into account the season, the time of the meal and a host of other variables.

That said, Indian cuisine is astonishingly varied and probably has a greater palette of flavours and seasonings than almost any other in the world. Indians love eating out and the range of eating places in city centres is very wide. Much of the best cooking, however, takes place within the home where recipes were traditionally handed down unwritten from generation to generation. Nowadays, more and more recipes are being recorded as food writers, cookery school owners and chefs travel the world in search of inspiration.

Thanks to long-haul travel, the wide availability of exotic ingredients and our fascination with spicy foods, Indian dishes have found a permanent place on the menu in both Europe and in the United States. Chicken Tikka Masala, though not strictly Indian, is a typical example, as are Lamb Rogan Josh and Tandoori Prawns. The number of Indian takeaways now exceeds that of their Chinese counterparts, and modern Indian restaurants abroad, with their high levels of cooking, are a far cry from the curry houses of the 1960s and 70s.

Indian Regional Cooking

With India's vast size and radical variations in topography and climate, the cuisine is highly regional. The diversity is most obvious in the contrast between the rich meat-based dishes of the northern states of Punjab, Kashmir and Uttar Pradesh, and the vegetarian and fish-based cuisine of the south, where rice is the staple food.

Different religions, each with a strict dietary code, also have a strong influence. Muslims do not eat pork as it is considered unclean, nor are they supposed to drink alcohol. Those Hindus who are not vegetarians do not eat beef, and nor do Sikhs.

Invasions by colonizers have shaped the cuisine too. Intrepid explorers from Portugal established Christian communities in south-west India and, as a result, the classic Pork Vindaloo found its way into Goan cuisine. In the days of the Raj, patient Indian cooks created mulligatawny soup for homesick British colonials, though soup was not previously part of their culinary repertoire.

The Indian Meal

In Indian homes all the dishes are usually served together rather than as separate courses, although modern Indians sometimes serve soup as a first course. The dishes may be served in communal bowls, or each person may have their own thali – a large metal plate with individual bowls (katori) on it – or a huge banana leaf on which portions of each dish are arranged.

It is customary for Indians to use the fingertips of the right hand, rather than cutlery, to scoop up food, except possibly when entertaining Western guests. It is unacceptable to eat with the left hand as it is considered unclean.

A meal at home might consist of a meat or fish dish, one or two vegetable dishes including pulses and a large bowl of rice or freshly baked flatbread, with chutney or fresh relishes as an accompaniment. Vegetarian menus will include a greater choice of vegetables and pulses.

Meals are sometimes rounded off with a selection of chilled sliced fruit, although on special occasions a rich dessert such as Shrikhand or a spicy rice pudding might be served.

What to drink

Most Indians drink water with a meal rather than alcohol, which is usually enjoyed before the meal, accompanied by tasty snacks such as Plantain Chips, deep-fried fritters or samosas. Where alcohol is forbidden, fruit juices and cordials are popular. Sweet or Salted Lassi, an iced drink made with lightly spiced yogurt, is the preferred drink in northern regions. Ginger Cordial and lime soda, seasoned with sugar and black pepper, are served all over India and are particularly thirst-quenching in the blistering heat.

Tips on Menu Planning

Planning an Indian meal is not so very different from organizing a well-balanced Western-style meal.

- Contrasting textures are important, as are a balance of rich, plain, hot and cooling foods.
- Always include bread, pulses or rice.
- Pungent relishes and chutneys perk up the appetite and aid digestion.
- Include a yogurt-based sauce to tame the heat.
- For a special meal add more meat and vegetable dishes, a larger selection of chutneys and perhaps a salad.
- Chosen carefully, wine can accompany an Indian meal, but chilled beer or lager is a safer bet.

Cooking Techniques

Most Indian cooking is done on top of the stove rather than in the oven. The following basic techniques are not difficult but are worth mastering.

Shallow-frying

Less common in India than deep-frying, and mainly used for pancakes and certain breads. Use just enough clean vegetable oil or ghee to stop the food sticking. The fat must be hot enough to brown the food gradually, but should not be smoking or hazy.

Deep-frying

Widely used in Indian cooking. For success use clean groundnut oil or ghee, both of which reach a high temperature without burning. The oil should be deep enough to cover the food and very hot, so that a morsel of uncooked food sizzles immediately.

Fry in small batches – crowding causes the temperature of the oil to drop, resulting in soggy food. Remove cooked food with tongs and drain well on paper towels. Always serve deep-fried foods piping hot.

Griddling

Griddling is a technique for cooking flat discs of wholemeal dough known as chapatis. Brush a tava (see Cooking Equipment) with a little fat and place over a medium heat. To test the temperature, sprinkle with a few drops of water, which should splatter when the tava is the correct heat.

Preparing and cooking spices

Once ground or crushed, spices quickly lose their distinctive flavours and aromas. Whole spices are a must, therefore, if you want bright zesty flavours. Indian cooks coax out maximum flavour by dry-frying whole spices without any oil. The spices are ready when they smell toasty and start to jump around the pan. Once toasted, spices can be ground to a paste with wet ingredients and used as a marinade or to thicken sauces.

Tempering is another flavouring technique in which whole spices are quickly fried in a little hot oil or ghee before the rest of the ingredients are added.

Bhagar is similar to tempering and is used to perk up bland food. Sizzled spices and oil are poured over just before serving. The dish is kept covered to retain all the fragrant aromas.

Cooking Equipment

Indian cooks use equipment similar to that found in Western kitchens. However, the following items will also come in handy.

Karahi

A bowl-shaped iron or steel pan with sloping walls, a rounded base and two ear-shaped handles. Used for deep-frying, shallow-frying and simmering. A wide saucepan with flared sides or a Chinese wok will work just as well.

Mortar and pestle

Every Indian kitchen has at least one mortar and pestle for grinding, crushing or mashing spices, pastes and other ingredients.

Spice grinder

Indians use a special flat stone but a small electric coffee grinder is more convenient. Remember to keep it solely for spices, as the flavour will permeate other foods.

Tandoor oven

A traditional clay oven built into the ground. The food is slapped directly on to the clay walls or is speared on skewers that rest against the sides. The food cooks in the intense heat, and the juices drip onto the coals, producing the characteristic smoky flavour. The technique is almost impossible to recreate, but reasonable results can be achieved with a covered barbecue.

Tava

A slightly concave metal disc with a long handle, used for cooking flat breads such as chapattis. A cast-iron griddle or non-stick crêpe pan make good substitutes.

Velan

A slim rolling pin for making flat breads. It is thicker in the middle to help flatten any uneven dough. A Western-style rolling pin can be used instead.

Ingredients

It's really easy nowadays to create authentic-tasting Indian food, thanks to the exciting range of exotic ingredients found in supermarkets and Asian food shops. The following are the most commonly used.

AMCHOOR

A powder with a sour flavour made from sun-dried, unripe mangoes.

ASAFOETIDA

An odd-smelling yellow powder that adds an onion-like flavour to vegetable dishes.

BASMATI RICE

The long-grain fragrant rice used throughout India and known the world over.

CARDAMOM PODS

Green: highly aromatic seeds in a small green or cream husk. Used to flavour sweet and savoury dishes.

Black: large brown paper husk. Seeds have a strong flavour and are used sparingly in spice mixes.

CHILLIES

Widely used in Indian cuisine: either fresh when unripe and green, or dried once red and ripe. Flavour ranges from mild to searingly hot.

COCONUT

Creamed: an oily compressed block that is crumbled into rich curries and soups.

Flakes, dried: Used as a crunchy garnish, or to add texture to salads and fresh relishes.

Fresh: sweet, nutty, crisp flesh that can be grated and pressed to produce milk.

Milk, canned: used instead of grated fresh coconut.

CORIANDER

Leaves: used freshly chopped as a distinctive flavouring and a garnish.

Seeds: used freshly ground as a seasoning and in spice mixes.

CUMIN SEEDS

Strongly pronounced flavour. Used whole or ground in spice mixes.

CURRY LEAVES

The leaves have a uniquely lemony, spicy and slightly bitter flavour – not at all like curry. Available dried or fresh. Fresh leaves freeze well and can be stored for months.

FENUGREEK

Very hard yellow seeds with a strong typically 'Indian' flavour. Also available as a powder.

GARAM MASALA

Originating from the cooler regions of northern India, a mix of spices that are believed to heat the body. There are many variations. Used mainly for seasoning meat, chicken and rice dishes.

GARLIC

Used extensively in curries, chopped finely and fried with onions, or processed to a paste. Garlic paste: peel and chop 1 head of garlic and blend to a paste with 2–3 tablespoons of water. Will keep for a week in the refrigerator.

GHEE

Butter that has been clarified to remove milk solids that would otherwise burn when heated. Used for all types of frying.

GINGER, FRESH

Used extensively in many Indian dishes, chopped finely or processed to a paste.

Ginger paste: peel and chop about 90 g/3¼ oz fresh ginger root and blend to a paste in a food processor with 2–3 tablespoons of water. Will keep for a week in the refrigerator.

MUSTARD OIL

Amber-coloured oil made from pressed mustard seeds. Briefly heated to a high temperature before use to tame the harsh mustardy flavour.

MUSTARD SEEDS

Reddish brown or black seeds with a mild nutty flavour that are usually sizzled in oil at the start of cooking.

NIGELLA SEEDS

Also called kalonji, jet-black seeds with a peppery flavour. Used in dhals and vegetable dishes and sprinkled on naan bread.

PANEER

Home-made fresh cheese made from milk curdled with lemon juice. Cut into cubes and fried with spices as a snack, or added to curries, vegetable dishes and salads.

PEPPERCORNS

Native to southern India and at one time the world's most important spice. Used in spice mixes and most Indian dishes.

PULSES

Protein-rich lentils, dried peas (dhal) and beans, used extensively throughout India.

SAFFRON

Red-orange stamens of the crocus plant. Always buy threads rather than ground powder. Has a unique highly aromatic flavour.

TAMARIND

A brown podded fruit with a sour flavour, compressed into sticky blocks of pulp that are soaked in water. Also sold as a concentrate that can be spooned straight from the jar.

TURMERIC

Originating from a rhizome but usually sold ground. Bright yellow powder with a musky, slightly bitter flavour. Essential in curries.

YOGURT

Gives body and creamy texture to curries and kormas. Also served as a cooling sauce mixed with spices, chopped cucumber or other vegetables.

Meat and Poultry

India boasts a fascinating choice of meat dishes, though the type of meat is often restricted by religion; Muslims do not eat pork, and non-vegetarian Hindus refrain from beef, as do Sikhs. Lamb is probably the most frequently used meat on the menu since it is free from dietary restrictions. Chicken comes a close second: it is versatile, cheap and as well suited to simmering in richly flavoured sauces as it is to roasting and grilling. Chickens in India are usually free-range and with a flavour far superior to battery-raised birds.

Curries are, of course, the most famous of Indian meat and poultry dishes, but they are by no means the only items in the Indian repertoire. There are delicately flavoured creamy kormas, dopiaza – a

variation of korma cooked with onion – and plenty of savoury meat and rice or lentil combinations. There are also incendiary pork vindaloo cooked with vinegar, marinated and skewered lamb brochettes, tasty meat balls cooked in various sauces and chicken roasted tandoori-style.

Even within this extensive choice, there are regional nuances that give a typical national dish distinctive flavour. South Indian curries, for example, are fierce and fiery, while in Kashmir and Punjab in the north they are comparatively mild. Western or Goan meat dishes are slow-cooked, spicy and thickened with coconut milk. In the East, sharp acidic flavours of tamarind, lime and green mangoes are typical.

Lamb Pasanda

SERVES 4–6

600 g/1 lb 5 oz boneless shoulder or leg of lamb
2 tbsp garlic and ginger purée
55 g/2 oz ghee or 4 tbsp vegetable or groundnut oil
3 large onions, chopped
1 fresh green chilli, deseeded and chopped
2 green cardamom pods, bruised
1 cinnamon stick, broken in half
2 tsp ground coriander
1 tsp ground cumin
1 tsp ground turmeric
250 ml/9 fl oz water
150 ml/5 fl oz double cream
4 tbsp ground almonds
1½ tsp salt
1 tsp garam masala
paprika and toasted flaked almonds, to garnish

1. Cut the meat into thin slices, then place the slices between clingfilm and pound with a meat mallet to make them even thinner. Put the lamb slices in a bowl, add the garlic and ginger paste and rub well into the lamb. Cover and leave to marinate in the refrigerator for 2 hours.

2. Melt the ghee in a large frying pan over a medium–high heat. Add the onions and chilli and cook, stirring frequently, for 5–8 minutes, until golden brown.

3. Stir in the cardamom pods, cinnamon stick, ground coriander, cumin and turmeric and continue stirring for 2 minutes, or until the spices are aromatic.

4. Add the meat to the pan and cook, stirring occasionally, for about 5 minutes, until it is brown on all sides and the fat begins to separate. Stir in the water and bring to the boil, still stirring. Reduce the heat to its lowest setting, cover the pan tightly and simmer for 40 minutes, or until the meat is tender.

5. Mix together the cream and ground almonds in a bowl. Beat in 6 tablespoons of the hot cooking liquid from the pan, then gradually beat this mixture back into the pan. Stir in the salt and garam masala. Continue to simmer for a further 5 minutes, uncovered, stirring occasionally.

6. Garnish with a sprinkling of paprika and flaked almonds and serve.

Lamb Rogan Josh

SERVES 4

350 ml/12 fl oz natural yogurt

½ tsp ground asafoetida, dissolved in 2 tbsp water

700 g/1 lb 9 oz boneless leg of lamb, trimmed and cut into 5-cm/2-inch cubes

2 tomatoes, deseeded and chopped

1 onion, chopped

25 g/1 oz ghee or 2 tbsp vegetable or groundnut oil

1½ tbsp garlic and ginger purée

2 tbsp tomato purée

2 bay leaves

1 tbsp ground coriander

¼–1 tsp chilli powder, ideally Kashmiri chilli powder

½ tsp ground turmeric

1 tsp salt

½ tsp garam masala

1. Put the yogurt in a large bowl and stir in the dissolved asafoetida. Add the lamb and use your hands to rub in all the marinade, then set aside for 30 minutes.

2. Meanwhile, put the tomatoes and onion in a blender and process until combined. Melt the ghee in a flameproof casserole or large frying pan with a tight-fitting lid. Add the garlic and ginger purée and stir around until the aromas are released.

3. Stir in the tomato mixture, tomato purée, bay leaves, coriander, chilli powder and turmeric, reduce the heat to low and simmer, stirring occasionally, for 5–8 minutes.

4. Add the lamb and salt with any leftover marinade and stir for 2 minutes. Cover, reduce the heat to low and simmer, stirring occasionally, for 30 minutes. The lamb should give off enough moisture to prevent it from catching on the base of the pan, but if the sauce looks too dry, stir in a little water.

5. Sprinkle with the garam masala, re-cover the pan and continue simmering for 15–20 minutes, until the lamb is tender. Serve immediately.

Lamb Dhansak

SERVES 4–6

700 g/1 lb 9 oz boneless shoulder of lamb, trimmed and cut into 5-cm/2-inch cubes
1 tbsp garlic and ginger purée
5 green cardamom pods
200 g/7 oz yellow lentils (toor dhal)
100 g/3½ oz pumpkin, peeled, deseeded and chopped
1 carrot, thinly sliced
1 fresh green chilli, deseeded and chopped
1 tsp fenugreek powder
500 ml/18 fl oz water
1 large onion, thinly sliced
30 g/1 oz ghee or 2 tbsp vegetable or groundnut oil
2 garlic cloves, crushed
salt
chopped fresh coriander, to garnish

DHANSAK MASALA
1 tsp garam masala
½ tsp ground coriander
½ tsp ground cumin
½ tsp chilli powder
½ tsp ground turmeric
¼ tsp ground cardamom
¼ tsp ground cloves

1. Put the lamb and 1 teaspoon of salt in a large saucepan with enough water to cover and bring to the boil. Reduce the heat and simmer, skimming the surface as necessary until no more foam rises. Stir in the garlic and ginger purée and cardamom pods and continue simmering for a total of 30 minutes.

2. Meanwhile, put the lentils, pumpkin, carrot, chilli and fenugreek powder in a large heavy-based saucepan and pour over the water. Bring to the boil, stirring occasionally, then reduce the heat and simmer for 20–30 minutes, until the lentils and carrot are tender. Stir in a little extra water if the lentils look as though they will catch on the base of the pan.

3. Leave the lentil mixture to cool slightly, then pour it into a food processor or blender and whizz until a thick, smooth sauce forms.

4. While the lamb and lentils are cooking, put the onion in a bowl, sprinkle with 1 teaspoon of salt and leave to stand for about 5 minutes. Use your hands to squeeze out the moisture.

5. Melt the ghee in a flameproof casserole or large frying pan with a tight-fitting lid over a high heat. Add the onion and cook, stirring constantly, for 2 minutes. Remove one third of the onion and continue frying the rest for a further 1–2 minutes, until golden brown. Using a slotted spoon, immediately remove the onion from the pan, as it will continue to darken as it cools.

6. Return the one third of the onion to the pan with the garlic. Stir in all the dhansak masala ingredients and cook for 2 minutes, stirring constantly. Add the cooked lamb and stir for a further 2 minutes. Add the lentil sauce and simmer over a medium heat to warm through, stirring and adding a little extra water, if needed. Adjust the seasoning, if necessary. Sprinkle with the remaining onion and serve, garnished with coriander.

Meatballs in Creamy Cashew Nut Sauce

SERVES 4

450 g/1 lb fresh lean lamb mince
1 tbsp thick set natural yogurt
1 egg, beaten
½ tsp ground cardamom
½ tsp ground nutmeg
½ tsp pepper
½ tsp dried mint
½ tsp salt, or to taste
300 ml/10 fl oz water
2.5-cm/1-inch piece cinnamon stick
5 green cardamom pods
5 cloves
2 bay leaves

3 tbsp sunflower or olive oil
1 onion, finely chopped
2 tsp garlic purée
1 tsp ground ginger
1 tsp ground fennel seeds
½ tsp ground turmeric
½–1 tsp chilli powder
125 g/4½ oz raw cashew nuts, soaked in 150 ml/5 fl oz boiling water for 20 minutes
150 ml/5 fl oz double cream
1 tbsp crushed pistachio nuts, to garnish

1. Put the lamb mince in a mixing bowl and add the yogurt, egg, cardamom, nutmeg, pepper, mint and salt. Knead the mince until it is smooth and velvety. Chill for 30–40 minutes, then divide into quarters. Make five balls out of each quarter and roll them between your palms to make them smooth and neat.

2. Bring the water to the boil in a large shallow pan and add all the whole spices and the bay leaves. Arrange the meatballs in a single layer in the spiced liquid, reduce the heat to medium, cover the pan and cook for 12–15 minutes. Remove the meatballs, cover and keep hot. Strain the spiced stock and set aside.

3. Wipe out the pan and add the oil. Place over a medium heat and add the onion and garlic purée. Cook until the mixture begins to brown and add the ground ginger, ground fennel seeds, turmeric and chillli powder. Stir-fry for 2–3 minutes, then add the strained stock and meatballs. Bring to the boil, reduce the heat to low, cover and simmer for 10–12 minutes.

4. Meanwhile, purée the cashews in a blender and add to the meatball mixture along with the cream. Simmer for a further 5–6 minutes, then remove from the heat. Garnish with crushed pistachio nuts and serve.

Marinated Lamb Brochettes

SERVES 4

700 g/1 lb 9 oz boned leg of lamb, cut into 2.5-cm/1-inch cubes

2 tbsp light malt vinegar

½ tsp salt, or to taste

1 tbsp garlic purée

1 tbsp ginger purée

115 g/4 oz whole milk natural yogurt, strained, or Greek-style yogurt

1 tbsp gram flour

1 tsp ground cumin

1 tsp garam masala

½–1 tsp chilli powder

½ tsp ground turmeric

3 tbsp olive or sunflower oil, plus 1 tbsp for brushing

½ red pepper, deseeded and cut into 2.5-cm/1-inch pieces

½ green pepper, deseeded and cut into 2.5-cm/1-inch pieces

8 shallots, halved

55 g/2 oz butter, melted

lemon wedges, to serve

1. Put the meat in a large non-metallic bowl and add the vinegar and salt and the garlic and ginger purées. Mix together thoroughly, cover and leave to marinate in the refrigerator for 30 minutes.

2. Put the yogurt and gram flour in a separate bowl and beat together with a fork until smooth. Add the cumin, garam masala, chilli powder, turmeric and oil and mix together thoroughly. Add the yogurt mixture to the marinated meat, then add the peppers and shallots and stir until well blended. Cover and leave to marinate in the refrigerator for 2–3 hours, or overnight. Return to room temperature before cooking.

3. Preheat the grill to high. Line the grill pan with a piece of foil. Brush the rack and 4 metal skewers with oil.

4. Thread the marinated lamb, peppers and shallots alternately onto the prepared skewers. Place the skewers on the prepared rack and cook under the preheated grill for 4 minutes. Brush generously with half the melted butter and cook for a further 2 minutes. Turn over and cook for 3–4 minutes. Brush with the remaining butter and cook for a further 2 minutes.

5. Balance the brochettes over a large saucepan or frying pan and leave to rest for 5–6 minutes before sliding off the skewers with a knife. Serve with the lemon wedges.

Kashmiri Lamb Chops

SERVES 4

4 lamb chump chops or 8 cutlets
300 ml/10 fl oz milk
1 tbsp ginger purée
½ tsp pepper
pinch of saffron threads, pounded
1½ tsp ground fennel seeds
1 tsp ground cumin
½ tsp chilli powder
4 cloves
2.5-cm/1-inch piece cinnamon stick
4 green cardamom pods, bruised
1 tsp salt, or to taste
½ tsp garam masala
1 tbsp fresh mint leaves, chopped, or ½ tsp dried mint
1 tbsp chopped fresh coriander leaves
mixed salad leaves, to serve

1. Remove the rind from the chops. Bring enough water to cover the chops to the boil in a medium saucepan. Add the chops, return to the boil and cook for 2–3 minutes. Drain the chops, rinse and drain again.

2. Put the drained chops into a large non-stick saucepan and add all the remaining ingredients, except the garam masala and herbs. Place the saucepan over a medium heat and stir until the milk begins to bubble. Reduce the heat to low, cover and cook for 30 minutes, turning the chops occasionally.

3. Remove from the heat. Using tongs, lift the chops out of the saucepan and shake the cooking liquid into a bowl. Strain the liquid and return to the saucepan with the chops. Cook over a medium heat, turning frequently, for 7–8 minutes, until the liquid has evaporated and the chops are browned.

4. Sprinkle the garam masala evenly over the chops and add the mint and coriander. Stir and cook for 1 minute. Serve immediately with a mixed salad.

Kheema Matar

SERVES 4–6

- 30 g/1 oz ghee or 2 tbsp vegetable or groundnut oil
- 2 tsp cumin seeds
- 1 large onion, finely chopped
- 1 tbsp garlic and ginger purée
- 2 bay leaves
- 1 tsp mild, medium or hot curry powder, to taste
- 2 tomatoes, deseeded and chopped
- 1 tsp ground coriander
- ¼–½ tsp chilli powder
- ¼ tsp ground turmeric
- pinch of sugar
- ½ teaspoon salt
- ½ teaspoon pepper
- 500 g/1 lb 2 oz fresh lean lamb or beef mince
- 250 g/9 oz frozen peas, straight from the freezer

1. Melt the ghee in a flameproof casserole or large frying pan with a tight-fitting lid. Add the cumin seeds and cook, stirring, for 30 seconds, or until they start to crackle.

2. Stir in the onion, garlic and ginger purée, bay leaves and curry powder and continue to stir-fry until the fat separates.

3. Stir in the tomatoes and cook for 1–2 minutes. Stir in the coriander, chilli powder, turmeric, sugar, salt and pepper and continue stirring for 30 seconds.

4. Add the lamb and cook for 5 minutes, or until it is no longer pink, using a wooden spoon to break up the meat. Reduce the heat and simmer, stirring occasionally, for 10 minutes.

5. Add the peas and continue simmering for a further 10–15 minutes, until the peas are thawed and hot. If there is too much liquid left in the pan, increase the heat and let it bubble for a few minutes until it reduces.

Beef Madras

SERVES 4–6

1–2 dried red chillies
2 tsp ground coriander
2 tsp ground turmeric
1 tsp black mustard seeds
½ tsp ground ginger
¼ tsp pepper
140 g/5 oz creamed coconut, grated and dissolved in 300 ml/10 fl oz boiling water
55 g/2 oz ghee or 4 tbsp vegetable or groundnut oil
2 onions, chopped
3 large garlic cloves, chopped
700 g/1 lb 9 oz lean stewing steak, such as chuck, trimmed and cut into 5-cm/2-inch cubes
250 ml/9 fl oz beef stock
lemon juice
salt
poppadoms, to serve

1. Depending on how hot you want this dish to be, chop the chillies with or without any seeds. The more seeds you include, the hotter the dish will be. Put the chopped chilli and any seeds in a small bowl with the coriander, turmeric, mustard seeds, ginger and pepper and stir in a little of the dissolved creamed coconut to make a thin paste.

2. Melt the ghee in a flameproof casserole or large frying pan with a tight-fitting lid over a medium–high heat. Add the onions and garlic and cook for 5–8 minutes, stirring frequently, until the onions are golden brown. Add the spice paste and stir around for 2 minutes, or until you can smell the aromas.

3. Add the meat and stock and bring to the boil. Reduce the heat to its lowest level, cover tightly and simmer for 1½ hours, or until the beef is tender. Check occasionally that the meat isn't catching on the base of the pan and stir in a little extra water or stock, if necessary.

4. Uncover the pan and stir in the remaining dissolved coconut cream with the lemon juice and salt to taste. Bring to the boil, stirring, then reduce the heat again and simmer, still uncovered, until the sauce reduces slightly. Serve with poppadoms.

Balti Beef

SERVES 4–6

30 g/1 oz ghee or 2 tbsp vegetable or groundnut oil
1 large onion, chopped
2 garlic cloves, crushed
2 large red peppers, deseeded and chopped
600 g/1 lb 5 oz boneless beef, such as sirloin, thinly sliced
fresh coriander sprigs, to garnish
Indian bread, to serve

BALTI SAUCE
30 g/1 oz ghee or 2 tbsp vegetable or groundnut oil
2 large onions, chopped
1 tbsp garlic and ginger purée
400 g/14 oz canned chopped tomatoes
1 tsp ground paprika
½ tsp ground turmeric
½ tsp ground cumin
½ tsp ground coriander
¼ tsp chilli powder
¼ tsp ground cardamom
1 bay leaf
salt and pepper

1. To make the balti sauce, melt the ghee in a wok or large frying pan over a medium–high heat. Add the onions and garlic and ginger purée and stir-fry for about 5 minutes, until the onions are golden brown. Stir in the tomatoes, then add the paprika, turmeric, cumin, coriander, chilli powder, cardamom, bay leaf and salt and pepper to taste. Bring to the boil, stirring, then reduce the heat and simmer for 20 minutes, stirring occasionally.

2. Leave the sauce to cool slightly, then remove the bay leaf and pour the mixture into a food processor or blender and whizz to a smooth sauce.

3. Wipe out the wok and return it to a medium–high heat. Add the ghee and melt. Add the onion and garlic and stir-fry for 5–8 minutes, until golden brown. Add the red peppers and continue stir-frying for 2 minutes.

4. Stir in the beef and continue stirring for 2 minutes, until it starts to turn brown. Add the balti sauce and bring to the boil. Reduce the heat and simmer for 5 minutes, or until the sauce slightly reduces again and the peppers are tender. Adjust the seasoning, if necessary. Garnish with coriander sprigs and serve with Indian bread.

Pork with Cinnamon and Fenugreek

SERVES 4

1 tsp ground coriander
1 tsp ground cumin
1 tsp chilli powder
1 tbsp dried fenugreek leaves
1 tsp ground fenugreek
150 ml/5 fl oz natural yogurt
450 g/1 lb diced pork fillet
4 tbsp ghee or vegetable oil
1 large onion, sliced
5-cm/2-inch piece fresh ginger, finely chopped
4 garlic cloves, finely chopped
1 cinnamon stick
6 green cardamom pods
6 whole cloves
2 bay leaves
175 ml/6 fl oz water
salt

1. Mix together the coriander, cumin, chilli powder, dried fenugreek, ground fenugreek and yogurt in a small bowl. Place the pork in a large, shallow non-metallic dish and add the spice mixture, turning well to coat. Cover with clingfilm and leave to marinate in the refrigerator for 30 minutes.

2. Melt the ghee in a large heavy-based saucepan. Cook the onion over a low heat, stirring occasionally, for 5 minutes, or until soft. Add the ginger, garlic, cinnamon stick, cardamom pods, cloves and bay leaves and cook, stirring constantly, for 2 minutes, or until the spices give off their aroma. Add the meat with its marinade and the water, and season to taste with salt. Bring to the boil, reduce the heat, cover and simmer for 30 minutes.

3. Transfer the meat mixture to a preheated wok or large heavy-based frying pan and cook over a low heat, stirring constantly, until dry and tender. If necessary, sprinkle occasionally with a little water to prevent it from sticking to the wok. Serve immediately.

Pork Vindaloo

SERVES 4–6

4 tbsp mustard oil
2 large onions, finely chopped
6 bay leaves
6 cloves
6 garlic cloves, chopped
3 green cardamom pods, lightly cracked
1–2 small fresh red chillies, chopped
2 tbsp ground cumin
½ tsp salt
½ tsp ground turmeric
2 tbsp cider vinegar
2 tbsp water
1 tbsp tomato purée
700 g/1 lb 9 oz boneless shoulder of pork, trimmed and cut into 5-cm/2-inch cubes

1. Put the mustard oil in a large frying pan or saucepan with a tight-fitting lid over a high heat until it smokes. Turn off the heat and leave the mustard oil to cool completely.

2. Reheat the oil over a medium–high heat. Add the onions and cook, stirring frequently, for 5–8 minutes until soft but not coloured.

3. Add the bay leaves, cloves, garlic, cardamom pods, chillies, cumin, salt, turmeric and 1 tablespoon of the vinegar to the onions and stir around. Stir in the water, then cover the pan and simmer for about 1 minute, or until the water is absorbed and the fat separates.

4. Dissolve the tomato purée in the remaining vinegar, then stir it into the pan. Add the pork and stir around.

5. Add just enough water to cover the pork and bring to the boil. Reduce the heat to its lowest level, cover the pan tightly and simmer for 40–60 minutes, until the pork is tender.

6. If too much liquid remains in the pan when the pork is tender, use a slotted spoon to remove the pork from the pan and boil the liquid until it reduces to the required amount. Return the pork to the pan to heat through, then transfer to warmed dishes and serve.

Chicken Tikka Masala

SERVES 4–6

400 g/14 oz canned chopped tomatoes
300 ml/10 fl oz double cream
1 cooked tandoori chicken, cut into 8 pieces
salt and pepper
fresh chopped coriander, to garnish
freshly cooked basmati rice, to serve

TIKKA MASALA
30 g/1 oz ghee or 2 tbsp vegetable or groundnut oil
1 large garlic clove, finely chopped
1 fresh red chilli, deseeded and chopped
2 tsp ground cumin
2 tsp ground paprika
½ tsp salt
pepper

1. To make the tikka masala, melt the ghee in a large frying pan with a tight-fitting lid over a medium heat. Add the garlic and chilli and stir-fry for 1 minute. Stir in the cumin, paprika, salt and pepper to taste and continue stirring for about 30 seconds.

2. Stir the tomatoes and cream into the pan. Reduce the heat to low and leave the sauce to simmer for about 10 minutes, stirring frequently, until it reduces and thickens.

3. Meanwhile, remove all the bones and any skin from the tandoori chicken pieces, then cut the meat into bite-sized pieces.

4. Adjust the seasoning of the sauce, if necessary. Add the chicken pieces to the pan, cover and leave to simmer for 3–5 minutes, until the chicken is heated through. Garnish with coriander and serve with freshly cooked basmati rice.

Pistachio Chicken Korma

SERVES 4

115 g/4 oz shelled pistachio nuts
200 ml/7 fl oz boiling water
good pinch of saffron threads, pounded
2 tbsp hot milk
700 g/1 lb 9 oz skinless, boneless chicken breasts or thighs, cut into 2.5-cm/1-inch cubes
1 tsp salt, or to taste
½ tsp pepper
juice of ½ lemon
55 g/2 oz ghee or unsalted butter
6 green cardamom pods
1 large onion, finely chopped
2 tsp garlic purée
2 tsp ginger purée
1 tbsp ground coriander
½ tsp chilli powder
280 g/10 oz whole milk natural yogurt, whisked
150 ml/5 fl oz single cream
2 tbsp rosewater
6–8 white rose petals, washed, to garnish
freshly cooked basmati rice and lemon wedges, to serve

1. Soak the pistachio nuts in the boiling water in a heatproof bowl for 20 minutes. Meanwhile, soak the pounded saffron in the hot milk.

2. Put the chicken in a non-metallic bowl and add the salt, pepper and lemon juice. Rub into the chicken, cover and leave to marinate in the refrigerator for 30 minutes.

3. Melt the ghee in a medium heavy-based saucepan over a low heat and add the cardamom pods. When they have puffed up, add the onion and increase the heat to medium. Cook, stirring frequently, for 8–9 minutes, until the onion is a pale golden colour.

4. Add the garlic and ginger purées and cook, stirring frequently, for a further 2–3 minutes. Add the coriander and chilli powder and cook, stirring, for 30 seconds. Add the chicken, increase the heat to medium–high and cook, stirring constantly, for 5–6 minutes, until it changes colour.

5. Reduce the heat to low and add the yogurt and the saffron and milk mixture. Bring to a slow simmer, cover and cook for 15 minutes. Stir halfway through to ensure that it does not stick to the base of the pan.

6. Meanwhile, put the pistachio nuts and their soaking water in a blender or food processor and process until smooth. Add to the chicken mixture, followed by the cream. Cover and simmer, stirring occasionally, for a further 15–20 minutes. Stir in the rosewater and remove from the heat. Garnish with the rose petals and serve immediately with freshly cooked basmati rice and lemon wedges.

Butter Chicken

SERVES 4–6

1 onion, chopped
1½ tbsp garlic and ginger purée
400 g/14 oz canned chopped tomatoes
¼–½ tsp chilli powder
pinch of sugar
30 g/1 oz ghee or 2 tbsp vegetable or groundnut oil
125 ml/4 fl oz water
1 tbsp tomato purée
40 g/1½ oz butter, cut into small pieces
½ tsp garam masala
½ tsp ground cumin
½ tsp ground coriander
8 cooked tandoori chicken pieces
4 tbsp double cream
salt and pepper
chopped cashew nuts and fresh coriander sprigs, to garnish

1. Put the onion and garlic and ginger purée in a food processor, blender or spice grinder and whizz together until a paste forms. Add the tomatoes, chilli powder, sugar and a pinch of salt and whizz again until blended.

2. Melt the ghee in a wok or large frying pan over a medium–high heat. Add the tomato mixture and water and stir in the tomato pureé.

3. Bring the mixture to the boil, stirring, then reduce the heat to low and simmer for 5 minutes, stirring occasionally, until the sauce thickens.

4. Stir in half the butter, the garam masala, cumin and coriander. Add the chicken pieces and stir around until they are well coated. Simmer for a further 10 minutes, or until the chicken is hot. Taste and adjust the seasoning, if necessary.

5. Lightly beat the cream in a small bowl and stir in several tablespoons of the hot sauce, beating constantly. Stir the cream mixture into the tomato sauce, then add the remaining butter and stir until it melts. Garnish with the chopped cashew nuts and coriander sprigs and serve straight from the pan.

Chicken Biryani

SERVES 4–5

85 g/3 oz whole milk natural yogurt
1 tbsp garlic purée
1 tbsp ginger purée
700 g/1 lb 9 oz skinless, boneless chicken thighs
1 tbsp white poppy seeds
2 tsp coriander seeds
½ mace blade
2 bay leaves, torn into small pieces
½ tsp black peppercorns
1 tsp green cardamom seeds
2.5-cm/1-inch piece cinnamon stick, broken up
4 cloves
55 g/2 oz ghee or unsalted butter
1 large onion, finely sliced
1½ tsp salt, or to taste

RICE
pinch of saffron threads, pounded
2 tbsp hot milk
1½ tsp salt
2 x 5-cm/2-inch cinnamon sticks
3 star anise
2 bay leaves, crumbled
4 cloves
4 green cardamom pods, bruised
450 g/1 lb basmati rice, washed

TO GARNISH
2 tbsp sunflower oil
1 onion, finely sliced

1. Put the yogurt and garlic and ginger purées in a bowl and beat together with a fork until thoroughly blended. Put the chicken in a non-metallic bowl, add the yogurt mixture and mix until well blended. Cover and leave to marinate in the refrigerator for 2 hours.

2. Grind the next 8 ingredients (all the seeds and spices) to a fine powder in a coffee grinder and set aside. In a flameproof casserole large enough to hold the chicken and the rice together, melt the ghee over a medium heat, add the onion and cook, stirring frequently, for 8–10 minutes, until a medium brown colour. Reduce the heat to low, add the ground ingredients and cook, stirring, for 2–3 minutes. Add the marinated chicken and salt and cook, stirring, for 2 minutes. Turn off the heat and keep the chicken covered.

3. To make the rice, soak the pounded saffron in the hot milk and set aside to soak for 20 minutes. Preheat the oven to 180°C/350°F/Gas Mark 4. Bring a large saucepan of water to the boil and add the salt and spices. Add the rice, return to the boil and boil steadily for 2 minutes. Drain the rice, reserving the whole spices, and pile on top of the chicken. Pour the saffron and milk over the rice.

4. Soak a piece of greaseproof paper large enough to cover the top of the rice completely and squeeze out the excess water. Lay on top of the rice. Soak a clean tea towel, wring out and lay loosely on top of the greaseproof paper. Cover the casserole with a piece of foil. It is important to cover the rice in this way to contain all the steam inside the casserole, as the biryani cooks entirely in the vapour created inside the casserole. Put the lid on top and cook in the centre of the preheated oven for 1 hour. Turn off the oven and leave the rice to stand inside for 30 minutes.

5. Meanwhile, heat the oil for the garnish in a small saucepan over a medium heat, add the onion and cook, stirring, for 12–15 minutes, until browned.

6. Transfer the biryani to a serving dish and garnish with the fried onions.

Chicken Dopiaza

SERVES 4

700 g/1 lb 9 oz skinless, boneless chicken breasts or thighs
juice of ½ lemon
1 tsp salt, or to taste
5 tbsp sunflower or olive oil
2 large onions, roughly chopped
5 large garlic cloves, roughly chopped
2.5-cm/1-inch piece fresh ginger, roughly chopped
2 tbsp whole milk natural yogurt
2.5-cm/1-inch piece cinnamon stick, halved
4 green cardamom pods, bruised
4 cloves
½ tsp black peppercorns
½ tsp ground turmeric
½–1 tsp chilli powder
1 tsp ground coriander
4 tbsp passata
150 ml/5 fl oz warm water
½ tsp granulated sugar
8 shallots, halved
1 tsp garam masala
2 tbsp chopped fresh coriander leaves
1 tomato, chopped
Indian bread, to serve

1. Cut the chicken into 2.5-cm/1-inch cubes and put in a non-metallic bowl. Add the lemon juice and half the salt and rub well into the chicken. Cover and leave to marinate in the refrigerator for 20 minutes.

2. Heat 1 tablespoon of the oil in a small saucepan over a medium heat, add the onions, garlic and ginger and cook, stirring frequently, for 4–5 minutes. Remove from the heat and leave to cool slightly. Transfer the ingredients to a blender or food processor, add the yogurt and blend to a purée.

3. Heat 3 tablespoons of the remaining oil in a medium heavy-based saucepan over a low heat, add the cinnamon stick, cardamom pods, cloves and peppercorns and cook, stirring, for 25–30 seconds. Add the puréed ingredients, increase the heat to medium and cook, stirring frequently, for 5 minutes.

4. Add the turmeric, chilli powder and ground coriander and cook, stirring, for 2 minutes. Add the passata and cook, stirring, for 3 minutes. Increase the heat slightly, then add the marinated chicken and cook, stirring, until it changes colour. Add the warm water, the remaining salt and the sugar. Bring to the boil, then reduce the heat to low, cover and cook for 10 minutes. Remove the lid and cook, uncovered, for a further 10 minutes, or until the sauce thickens.

5. Meanwhile, heat the remaining 1 tablespoon of oil in a small saucepan, add the shallots and stir-fry until browned and separated. Add the garam masala and cook, stirring, for 30 seconds. Stir the shallot mixture into the curry and simmer for 2 minutes. Stir in the fresh coriander and chopped tomato and remove from the heat. Serve immediately with Indian bread.

Chicken Jalfrezi

SERVES 4

700 g/1 lb 9 oz skinless, boneless chicken breasts or thighs
juice of ½ lemon
1 tsp salt, or to taste
5 tbsp sunflower or olive oil
1 large onion, finely chopped
2 tsp garlic purée
2 tsp ginger purée
½ tsp ground turmeric
1 tsp ground cumin
2 tsp ground coriander
½–1 tsp chilli powder
150 g/5½ oz canned chopped tomatoes
150 ml/5 fl oz warm water
1 large garlic clove, finely chopped
1 small or ½ large red pepper, deseeded and cut into 2.5-cm/1-inch pieces
1 small or ½ large green pepper, deseeded and cut into 2.5-cm/1-inch pieces
1 tsp garam masala
Indian bread or freshly cooked basmati rice, to serve

1. Cut the chicken into 2.5-cm/1-inch cubes and put in a non-metallic bowl. Add the lemon juice and half the salt and rub well into the chicken. Cover and leave to marinate in the refrigerator for 20 minutes.

2. Heat 4 tablespoons of the oil in a medium heavy-based saucepan over a medium heat. Add the onion and cook, stirring frequently, for 8–9 minutes, until lightly browned. Add the garlic and ginger pureés and cook, stirring, for 3 minutes. Add the turmeric, cumin, coriander and chilli powder and cook, stirring, for 1 minute. Add the tomatoes and cook for 2–3 minutes, stirring frequently, until the oil separates from the spice paste.

3. Add the marinated chicken, increase the heat slightly and cook, stirring, until it changes colour. Add the warm water and bring to the boil. Reduce the heat, cover and simmer for 25 minutes.

4. Heat the remaining 1 tablespoon of oil in a small saucepan or frying pan over a low heat. Add the garlic and cook, stirring frequently, until browned. Add the red and green peppers, increase the heat to medium and stir-fry for 2 minutes, then stir in the garam masala. Fold the pepper mixture into the curry. Remove from the heat and serve immediately with Indian bread.

Tandoori Chicken

SERVES 4

- 4 chicken pieces, about 225 g/8 oz each, skinned
- juice of ½ lemon
- ½ tsp salt, or to taste
- 85 g/3 oz whole milk natural yogurt, strained, or Greek-style yogurt
- 3 tbsp double cream
- 1 tbsp gram flour
- 1 tbsp garlic purée
- 1 tbsp ginger purée
- ½–1 tsp chilli powder
- 1 tsp ground coriander
- ½ tsp ground cumin
- ½ tsp garam masala
- ½ tsp ground turmeric
- vegetable oil, for brushing
- 3 tbsp melted butter or olive oil
- salad, to serve
- lemon wedges, to garnish

1. Make 2–3 small incisions in each chicken piece and place in a large non-metallic bowl. Rub in the lemon juice and salt, cover and chill in the refrigerator for 20 minutes.

2. Meanwhile, put the yogurt in a separate bowl and add the cream and gram flour. Beat with a fork until well blended and smooth. Add all the remaining ingredients, except the oil and melted butter, and mix thoroughly. Pour the over the chicken and rub in well. Cover and chill in the refrigerator for 4–6 hours, or overnight. Return to room temperature before cooking.

3. Preheat the grill to high. Line a grill pan with foil and brush the rack with oil. Using tongs, lift the chicken pieces out of the marinade and put on the prepared rack, reserving the remaining marinade. Cook the chicken under the preheated grill for 4 minutes, then turn over and cook for a further 4 minutes. Baste the chicken generously with the reserved marinade and cook for a further 2 minutes on each side.

4. Brush the chicken with the melted butter and cook for 5–6 minutes, or until charred in patches. Turn over and baste with the remaining marinade. Cook for a further 5–6 minutes, or until charred as before and the juices run clear when a skewer is inserted into the thickest part of the meat.

5. Transfer the chicken to a dish. Serve with salad and garnish with lemon wedges.

Silky Chicken Kebabs

SERVES 8

55 g/2 oz raw cashew nuts

2 tbsp single cream

1 egg

450 g/1 lb skinless, boneless chicken breasts, roughly chopped

½ tsp salt, or to taste

2 tsp garlic purée

2 tsp ginger purée

2 fresh green chillies, roughly chopped

15 g/½ oz fresh coriander, including the tender stalks, roughly chopped

1 tsp garam masala

vegetable oil, for brushing

25 g/1 oz butter, melted

chutney, to serve

1. Put the cashew nuts in a heatproof bowl, cover with boiling water and leave to soak for 20 minutes. Drain and put in a food processor. Add the cream and egg and process the ingredients to a coarse mixture.

2. Add all the remaining ingredients, except the oil and melted butter, and process until smooth. Transfer to a bowl, cover and chill in the refrigerator for 30 minutes.

3. Preheat the grill to high. Brush the rack and 8 metal or pre-soaked wooden skewers lightly with oil. Have a bowl of cold water ready.

4. Divide the chilled mixture into 8 equal-sized portions. Dip your hands into the bowl of cold water – this will stop the mixture sticking to your fingers when you are moulding it onto the skewers. Carefully mould each portion onto a skewer, forming it into a 15-cm/6-inch sausage shape. Arrange the kebabs on the prepared rack and cook under the preheated grill for 4 minutes. Brush with half the melted butter and cook for a further minute. Turn over and cook for 3 minutes. Baste with the remaining melted butter and cook for a further 2 minutes.

5. Remove from the heat and leave the kebabs to rest for 5 minutes before sliding them off the skewers with a knife. Serve with chutney.

Fish and Seafood

India has over 4,350 miles/7,000 km of coastline and numerous inland waterways, so it is not surprising that fish, seafood and fresh water fish feature largely on the menu in certain areas. Coastal regions from north to south boast a vast array of fish and seafood including some of the best crayfish in the world. Goan Seafood Curry and Balti Fish Curry are particularly worth trying. Mussels are also good especially when cooked Keralan-style in a coconut sauce.

North of Bengal towards Nepal, many rivers and steams flow down from the Himalayas. The icy water is clean and pure, and is home to a great variety of lake and river fish. The Bengalis consider these superior to marine fish since the flavour is thought to be cleaner and fresher.

Sometimes fish are grilled whole on the spit, a cooking method that produces a fabulous crisp skin and a moist and flaky interior.

Firm-fleshed fish may also be cut into chunks, sprinkled with a few spices and brushed with oil, then cooked on skewers as in Fish Tikka. Others are fried whole, sometimes coated in a spicy batter, or in fish and vegetable batter-coated fritters called pakoras.

Fish with a meaty texture, such as swordfish or cod is gently braised in spicy sauces often flavoured with coconut. Fish is also cooked in a rich tomato and chilli sauce with crispy fried onions.

Other cooking methods for fish are baking, steaming, poaching and roasting. Regardless of the method, all Indian fish dishes have that characteristic flavour that comes from a judicious mix of spices that enhances, but does not overwhelm, the delicate flavour of the fish.

Goan Fish Curry

SERVES 4

4 skinless salmon fillets, about 200 g/7 oz each
1 tsp salt, or to taste
1 tbsp lemon juice
3 tbsp sunflower or olive oil
1 large onion, finely chopped
2 tsp garlic purée
2 tsp ginger purée
½ tsp ground turmeric
1 tsp ground coriander
½ tsp ground cumin
½–1 tsp chilli powder
250 ml/9 fl oz canned coconut milk
2–3 fresh green chillies, sliced lengthways
2 tbsp cider vinegar or white wine vinegar
2 tbsp chopped fresh coriander leaves
freshly cooked basmati rice, to serve

1. Cut the salmon fillets in half and lay them on a flat surface in a single layer. Sprinkle with half the salt and the lemon juice and rub in gently. Cover and leave to marinate in the refrigerator for 15–20 minutes.

2. Heat the oil in a frying pan over a medium heat, add the onion and cook, stirring frequently to ensure even colouring, for 8–9 minutes, until a pale golden colour.

3. Add the garlic and ginger purées and cook, stirring, for 1 minute, then add the turmeric, ground coriander, cumin and chilli powder and cook, stirring, for 1 minute. Add the coconut milk, chillies and vinegar, then the remaining salt, stir well and simmer, uncovered, for 6–8 minutes.

4. Add the fish and cook gently for 5–6 minutes. Stir in the fresh coriander and remove from the heat. Serve immediately with freshly cooked basmati rice.

Fish Tikka

SERVES 4

pinch of saffron threads, pounded
1 tbsp hot milk
85 g/3 oz Greek-style yogurt
1 tbsp garlic purée
1 tbsp ginger purée
1 tsp salt, or to taste
½ tsp granulated sugar
juice of ½ lemon
½–1 tsp chilli powder
½ tsp garam masala
1 tsp ground fennel seeds
2 tsp gram flour
750 g/1 lb 10 oz salmon fillets, skinned and cut into 5-cm/2-inch cubes
3 tbsp olive oil, plus extra for brushing
sliced tomatoes and cucumber, to garnish
lemon wedges, to serve

1. Soak the pounded saffron in the hot milk for 10 minutes.

2. Put all the remaining ingredients, except the fish and oil, in a bowl and beat with a fork or a wire whisk until smooth. Stir in the saffron and milk, mix well and add the fish cubes. Using a metal spoon, mix gently, turning the fish around until fully coated with the marinade. Cover and leave to marinate in the refrigerator for 2 hours. Return to room temperature before cooking.

3. Preheat the grill to high. Brush a grill rack generously with oil and 8 metal skewers lightly with oil. Line the grill pan with a piece of foil.

4. Thread the fish cubes onto the prepared skewers, leaving narrow gaps between the pieces. Arrange on the prepared rack and cook under the preheated grill for 3 minutes. Brush half the oil over the kebabs and cook for a further minute. Turn over and brush any remaining marinade over the fish. Cook for 3 minutes. Brush the remaining oil over the fish and cook for a further 2 minutes, or until the fish is lightly charred.

5. Remove from the heat and leave to rest for 5 minutes. Garnish with tomatoes and cucumber and serve with lemon wedges for squeezing over.

Fish in Tomato and Chilli Sauce with Fried Onion

SERVES 4

700 g/1 lb 9 oz tilapia fillets, cut into 5-cm/2-inch pieces
2 tbsp lemon juice
1 tsp salt, or to taste
1 tsp ground turmeric
4 tbsp sunflower or olive oil, plus extra for shallow-frying
2 tsp granulated sugar
1 large onion, finely chopped
2 tsp ginger purée
2 tsp garlic purée
½ tsp ground fennel seeds
1 tsp ground coriander
½–1 tsp chilli powder
175 g/6 oz canned chopped tomatoes
300 ml/10 fl oz warm water
2–3 tbsp chopped fresh coriander leaves
freshly cooked basmati rice, to serve

1. Lay the fish on a plate and gently rub in the lemon juice, half the salt and half the turmeric. Set aside for 15–20 minutes.

2. Pour enough oil into a frying pan to cover its base to a depth of about 1 cm/½ inch and place over a medium–high heat. Fry the pieces of fish, in a single layer, until well browned on both sides. Drain on kitchen paper.

3. Heat the 4 tablespoons of oil in a medium saucepan over a medium heat and add the sugar. Allow it to brown but not to blacken, watching it carefully. Add the onion and cook for 5 minutes, until soft. Add the ginger and garlic purées, and cook for a further 3–4 minutes.

4. Add the ground fennel, ground coriander, chilli powder and remaining turmeric. Cook for about a minute, then add half the tomatoes. Cook until the tomato juice has evaporated, then add the remaining tomatoes. Continue to cook, stirring, until the oil separates from the spice paste.

5. Pour in the warm water and add the remaining salt. Bring to the boil, then add the fish, stir gently, and reduce the heat to low. Cook, uncovered, for 5–6 minutes, then stir in the chopped coriander and remove from the heat. Serve with freshly cooked basmati rice.

Fish Korma

SERVES 4

- 700 g/1 lb 9 oz tilapia fillets, cut into 5-cm/ 2-inch pieces
- 1 tbsp lemon juice
- 1 tsp salt
- 55 g/2 oz raw unsalted cashew nuts
- 3 tbsp sunflower or olive oil
- 5-cm/2-inch piece cinnamon stick, halved
- 4 green cardamom pods, bruised
- 2 cloves
- 1 large onion, finely chopped
- 1–2 fresh green chillies, chopped
- 2 tsp ginger purée
- 2 tsp garlic purée
- 150 ml/5 fl oz single cream
- 55 g/2 oz whole milk natural yogurt
- ¼ tsp ground turmeric
- ½ tsp sugar
- 1 tbsp toasted flaked almonds, to garnish
- Indian bread, to serve

1. Place the fish on a large plate and gently rub in the lemon juice and ½ teaspoon of the salt. Set aside for 20 minutes. Put the cashews in a bowl, cover with boiling water and leave to soak for 15 minutes.

2. Heat the oil in a wide shallow pan over a low heat and add the cinnamon, cardamom and cloves. Let them sizzle for 30–40 seconds.

3. Add the onion, chillies and ginger and garlic purées. Increase the heat slightly and cook, stirring frequently, for 9–10 minutes, until the onion is very soft.

4. Meanwhile, drain the cashews and purée them with the cream and yogurt.

5. Stir the turmeric into the onion mixture and add the puréed ingredients, the remaining salt and the sugar. Mix thoroughly and arrange the fish in the sauce in a single layer. Bring to a slow simmer, cover the pan and cook for 5 minutes. Remove the lid and shake the pan gently from side to side. Spoon some of the sauce over the pieces of fish. Re-cover and cook for a further 3–4 minutes.

6. Transfer to a serving dish and garnish with the toasted almonds. Serve with Indian bread.

Balti Fish Curry

SERVES 4–6

900 g/2 lb thick fish fillets, such as monkfish, grey mullet, cod or haddock, rinsed and cut into large chunks

2 bay leaves, torn

140 g/5 oz ghee or 150 ml/5 fl oz vegetable or groundnut oil

2 large onions, chopped

½ tbsp salt

150 ml/5 fl oz water

chopped fresh coriander, to garnish

Indian bread, to serve

MARINADE

½ tbsp garlic and ginger purée

1 fresh green chilli, deseeded and chopped

1 tsp ground coriander

1 tsp ground cumin

½ tsp ground turmeric

¼–½ tsp chilli powder

1 tbsp water

salt

1. To make the marinade, mix together the garlic and ginger purée, green chilli, ground coriander, cumin, turmeric and chilli powder with together with salt to taste in a large bowl. Gradually stir in the water to form a thin paste. Add the fish chunks and smear with the marinade. Tuck the bay leaves underneath and leave to marinate in the refrigerator for at least 30 minutes, or up to 4 hours.

2. Remove the fish from the refrigerator 15 minutes in advance of cooking. Melt the ghee in a wok or large frying pan over a medium–high heat. Add the onions, sprinkle with the salt and cook, stirring frequently, for 8 minutes, or until they are very soft and golden.

3. Gently add the fish to the pan with its marinade and the bay leaves, and stir in the water. Bring to the boil, then immediately reduce the heat and cook the fish for 4–5 minutes, spooning the sauce over the fish and carefully moving the chunks around until they are cooked through and the flesh flakes easily. Garnish with coriander and serve with Indian bread.

Bengali-style Fish

SERVES 4–6

- 1 tsp ground turmeric
- 1 tsp salt
- 1 kg/2 lb 4 oz cod fillet, skinned and cut into pieces
- 6 tbsp mustard oil
- 4 fresh green chillies
- 1 tsp finely chopped fresh ginger
- 1 tsp crushed garlic
- 2 onions, finely chopped
- 2 tomatoes, finely chopped
- 450 ml/16 fl oz water
- chopped fresh coriander, to garnish
- Indian bread, to serve

1. Mix together the turmeric and salt in a small bowl, then spoon the mixture over the fish pieces.
2. Heat the mustard oil in a large heavy-based frying pan. Add the fish and fry until pale yellow. Remove the fish with a slotted spoon and reserve.
3. Place the chillies, ginger, garlic, onions and tomatoes in a mortar and grind with a pestle to make a paste. Alternatively, place the ingredients in a food processor and process until smooth.
4. Transfer the spice paste to a clean frying pan and dry-fry until golden brown.
5. Remove the frying pan from the heat and place the fish pieces in the paste without breaking up the fish. Return the frying pan to the heat, add the water and cook over a medium heat for 15–20 minutes. Transfer to a warmed serving dish, garnish with chopped coriander and serve with Indian bread.

Steamed Fish with Coriander Chutney

SERVES 4

1 quantity of coriander chutney (see page 157)
1 large fresh banana leaf
vegetable or groundnut oil
4 white fish fillets, such as pomfret or sole, about 140 g/5 oz each
salt and pepper
lime or lemon wedges, to serve

1. Prepare the coriander chutney at least 2 hours in advance to allow the flavours to blend.
2. Meanwhile, cut the banana leaf into 4 squares large enough to fold comfortably around the fish to make tight parcels.
3. Working with one piece of leaf at a time, very lightly rub the bottom with oil. Put one of the fish fillets in the centre of the oiled side, flesh-side up. Spread one quarter of the coriander chutney over the top and season to taste with salt and pepper.
4. Fold one side of the leaf over the fish, then fold over the opposite side. Turn the leaf so the folded edges are top and bottom. Fold the right-hand end of the leaf parcel into the centre, then fold over the left-hand side. Trim the ends if the parcel becomes too bulky.
5. Use 2 wooden skewers to close the leaf parcel. Repeat with the remaining ingredients and banana leaf squares.
6. Place a steamer large enough to hold the parcels in a single layer over a pan of boiling water, without letting the water touch the fish. Add the fish, cover the pan and steam for 15 minutes. Make sure the fish is cooked through and flakes easily.
7. Serve the fish parcels with lime or lemon wedges.

Sole in Chilli Yogurt

SERVES 4

2 tbsp vegetable or groundnut oil
1 large onion, sliced
4-cm/1½-inch piece fresh ginger, finely chopped
½ tsp salt
¼ tsp ground turmeric
pinch of ground cinnamon
pinch of ground cloves
200 ml/7 fl oz natural yogurt
1 tbsp plain flour
small pinch of chilli powder
4 skinless sole fillets, about 150 g/5½ oz each, wiped dry
30 g/1 oz ghee or 2 tbsp vegetable or groundnut oil
salt and pepper
2 fresh fat green chillies, deseeded and finely chopped, to garnish

1. Heat the oil in a large frying pan over a medium–high heat. Add the onion and fry, stirring, for 8 minutes, or until it is soft and dark golden brown. Add the ginger and stir around for a further minute.

2. Stir in the salt, turmeric, cinnamon and cloves and continue stirring for 30 seconds. Remove the pan from the heat and stir in the yogurt, a little at a time, beating constantly.

3. Transfer the yogurt mixture to a blender or food processor and whizz until a paste forms.

4. Season the flour with chilli powder and salt and pepper to taste. Place it on a plate and use to dust the fish fillets lightly on both sides.

5. Wipe out the pan, then melt the ghee over a medium–high heat. When it is bubbling, reduce the heat to medium and add the fish fillets in a single layer. Fry for 2½ minutes, or until golden, then turn them over.

6. Continue frying for a further minute, then add the yogurt sauce to the pan and reheat, stirring. When the fillets flake easily and are cooked through and the sauce is hot, transfer to plates and sprinkle with the green chilli.

Fish Pakoras

SERVES 4

½ tsp salt

2 tbsp lemon juice or distilled white vinegar

700 g/1 lb 9 oz skinless white fish fillets, such as cod, halibut or monkfish, rinsed, patted dry and cut into large chunks

vegetable or groundnut oil, for deep-frying

pepper

lemon wedges, to serve

BATTER

140 g/5 oz gram flour

seeds from 4 green cardamom pods

large pinch of ground turmeric

large pinch of bicarbonate of soda

finely grated rind of 1 lemon

175 ml/6 fl oz water

salt and pepper

1. Combine the salt, lemon juice and pepper to taste and rub all over the fish chunks, then set aside in a non-metallic bowl and leave to stand for 20–30 minutes.

2. Meanwhile, to make the batter, put the gram flour in a bowl and stir in the seeds from the cardamom pods, the turmeric, bicarbonate of soda, lemon rind and salt and pepper to taste. Make a well in the centre and gradually stir in the water until a thin batter forms, similar in consistency to single cream. Gently stir the pieces of fish into the batter, taking care not to break them up.

3. Heat enough oil for deep-frying in a wok, deep-fat fryer or large heavy-based saucepan to 180°C/350°F, or until a cube of bread browns in 30 seconds. Remove the fish pieces from the batter and let the excess batter drip back into the bowl. Without overcrowding the pan, drop fish pieces in the hot oil and fry for about 2½–3 minutes, until golden brown.

4. Use a slotted spoon to remove the fried fish pieces from the oil and drain on crumpled kitchen paper. Continue until all the fish is fried, then serve hot with the lemon wedges.

Goan-style Seafood Curry

SERVES 4–6

3 tbsp vegetable or groundnut oil
1 tbsp black mustard seeds
12 fresh or 1 tbsp dried curry leaves
6 shallots, finely chopped
1 garlic clove, crushed
1 tsp ground turmeric
½ tsp ground coriander
¼–½ tsp chilli powder
140 g/5 oz creamed coconut, grated and dissolved in 300 ml/10 fl oz boiling water
500 g/1 lb 2 oz skinless, boneless white fish, such as monkfish or cod, cut into large chunks
450 g/1 lb large raw prawns, peeled and deveined
finely grated rind and juice of 1 lime
salt

1. Heat the oil in a wok or large frying pan over a high heat. Add the mustard seeds and stir them around for about 1 minute, or until they pop. Stir in the curry leaves.

2. Add the shallots and garlic and stir for about 5 minutes, or until the shallots are golden. Stir in the turmeric, coriander and chilli powder and continue stirring for about 30 seconds.

3. Add the dissolved creamed coconut. Bring to the boil, then reduce the heat to medium and stir for about 2 minutes.

4. Reduce the heat to low, add the fish and simmer for 1 minute, spooning the sauce over the fish and very gently stirring it around. Add the prawns and continue to simmer for a further 4–5 minutes, until the fish flakes easily and the prawns turn pink and curl.

5. Add half the lime juice, then taste and add more lime juice and salt to taste. Sprinkle with the lime rind and serve.

Prawn and Pineapple Tikka

SERVES 4

1 tsp cumin seeds
1 tsp coriander seeds
½ tsp fennel seeds
½ tsp yellow mustard seeds
¼ tsp fenugreek seeds
¼ tsp nigella seeds
pinch of chilli powder
2 tbsp lemon or pineapple juice
12 raw tiger prawns, peeled, deveined and tails left intact
12 bite-sized wedges of fresh or well-drained canned pineapple
salt
chopped fresh coriander, to garnish

1. Dry-roast the cumin, coriander, fennel, mustard, fenugreek and nigella seeds in a hot frying pan over a high heat, stirring them around constantly, until you can smell the aroma of the spices. Immediately tip the spices out of the pan so they do not burn, and reserve.

2. Put the spices in a spice grinder or mortar, add the chilli powder and salt to taste and grind to a fine powder. Transfer to a non-metallic bowl and stir in the lemon juice.

3. Add the prawns to the bowl and stir them around so they are well coated, then set aside to marinate for 10 minutes. Meanwhile, preheat the grill to high.

4. Thread 3 prawns and 3 pineapple wedges alternately onto metal or presoaked wooden skewers. Grill about 10 cm/4 inches from the heat for 2 minutes on each side, brushing with any leftover marinade, until the prawns turn pink and are cooked through.

5. Serve the prawns and pineapple wedges on the skewers with plenty of fresh coriander sprinkled over.

Tandoori Prawns

SERVES 4

4 tbsp natural yogurt
2 fresh green chillies, deseeded and chopped
½ tbsp garlic and ginger purée
seeds from 4 green cardamom pods
2 tsp ground cumin
1 tsp tomato purée
¼ tsp ground turmeric
¼ tsp salt
pinch of chilli powder, ideally Kashmiri chilli powder
24 raw tiger prawns, thawed if frozen, peeled, deveined and tails left intact
oil, for greasing
lemon or lime wedges, to serve

1. Put the yogurt, chillies and garlic and ginger purée in a small food processor or spice grinder and whizz until a paste forms. Transfer the paste to a large non-metallic bowl and stir in the cardamom seeds, cumin, tomato purée, turmeric, salt and chilli powder.

2. Add the prawns to the bowl and use your hands to make sure they are coated with the yogurt marinade. Cover the bowl with clingfilm and chill for at least 30 minutes, or up to 4 hours.

3. When you are ready to cook, heat a large griddle or frying pan over a high heat until a few drops of water 'dance' when they hit the surface. Use crumpled kitchen paper or a pastry brush to grease the hot pan very lightly with oil.

4. Use tongs to lift the prawns out of the marinade, letting the excess marinade drip back into the bowl, then place the prawns on the griddle and cook for 2 minutes. Flip the prawns over and cook for a further 1–2 minutes, until they turn pink, curl and are opaque all the way through when you cut one. Serve immediately with lemon wedges for squeezing over.

Prawn Pooris

SERVES 6

2 tsp coriander seeds
½ tsp black peppercorns
1 large garlic clove, crushed
1 tsp ground turmeric
¼–½ tsp chilli powder
½ tsp salt
40 g/1½ oz ghee or 3 tbsp vegetable or groundnut oil
1 onion, grated
800 g/1 lb 12 oz canned crushed tomatoes
pinch of sugar
500 g/1 lb 2 oz small cooked peeled prawns, thawed if frozen
½ tsp garam masala, plus extra to garnish
6 pooris, kept warm
fresh chopped coriander, to garnish

1. Put the coriander seeds, peppercorns, garlic, turmeric, chilli powder and salt in a small food processor, spice grinder or mortar and blend to a thick paste.

2. Melt the ghee in a wok or large frying pan over a medium–low heat. Add the paste and cook, stirring constantly, for about 30 seconds.

3. Add the grated onion and stir around for a further 30 seconds. Stir in the tomatoes and the sugar. Bring to the boil, stirring, and leave to bubble for 10 minutes, or until reduced, mashing the tomatoes against the side of the pan to break them down. Taste and add extra salt, if necessary.

4. Add the prawns and sprinkle with the garam masala. When the prawns are hot, arrange the warm pooris on plates and top each one with a portion of the prawns. Sprinkle with the coriander and garam masala and serve.

Mussels in Coconut Sauce

SERVES 4

1 kg/2 lb 4 oz live mussels, scrubbed and debearded

3 tbsp ghee or vegetable oil

1 onion, finely chopped

1 tsp garlic purée

1 tsp ginger purée

1 tsp ground cumin

1 tsp ground coriander

½ tsp ground turmeric

pinch of salt

600 ml/1 pint canned coconut milk

chopped fresh coriander, to garnish

1. Discard any mussels with broken shells and any that refuse to close when tapped with a knife. Set aside.

2. Heat the ghee in a large heavy-based frying pan. Add the onion and cook over a low heat, stirring occasionally, for 10 minutes, or until golden.

3. Add the garlic and ginger purées and cook, stirring constantly, for 2 minutes. Add the cumin, ground coriander, turmeric and salt and cook, stirring constantly, for a further 2 minutes. Stir in the coconut milk and bring to the boil.

4. Add the mussels, cover and cook for 5 minutes, or until the mussels have opened. Discard any mussels that remain closed. Transfer the mussels, with the coconut sauce, to a large warmed serving dish. Sprinkle with chopped coriander and serve immediately.

Mussels with Mustard Seeds and Shallots

SERVES 4

- 2 kg/4 lb 8 oz live mussels, scrubbed and debearded
- 3 tbsp vegetable or groundnut oil
- ½ tbsp black mustard seeds
- 8 shallots, chopped
- 2 garlic cloves, crushed
- 2 tbsp distilled vinegar
- 4 small fresh red chillies
- 85 g/3 oz creamed coconut, dissolved in 300 ml/10 fl oz boiling water
- 10 fresh or 1 tbsp dried curry leaves
- ½ tsp ground turmeric
- ¼–½ tsp chilli powder
- salt

1. Discard any mussels with broken shells and any that refuse to close when tapped with a knife. Set aside.

2. Heat the oil in a wok or large frying pan over a medium–high heat. Add the mustard seeds and stir them around for about 1 minute, or until they start to pop.

3. Add the shallots and garlic and cook, stirring frequently, for 3 minutes, or until they start to brown. Stir in the vinegar, whole chillies, dissolved creamed coconut, curry leaves, turmeric, chilli powder and a pinch of salt and bring to the boil, stirring.

4. Reduce the heat to very low. Add the mussels, cover the pan and leave to simmer, shaking the pan frequently, for 3–4 minutes, or until the mussels have opened. Discard any mussels that remain closed. Ladle the mussels into deep bowls, then taste the broth and add extra salt, if necessary. Spoon over the mussels and serve.

Vegetables and Pulses

Born of the centuries-old tradition of vegetarianism, Indian cooks weave their magic with vegetables and pulses, turning the simplest of fresh or dried produce into most spectacular feasts. Some of the cooking methods may be unfamiliar but they result in snacks and meals that are both a pleasure to eat and nourishing to the mind and body. Popular dishes are vegetable curries and kormas, fritters and bhajis, and thick lentil-based soups called sambars. Potatoes are always popular, particularly with spinach or cauliflower. Green beans and potatoes are another favourite combination.

The culture of vegetarianism is most strong in the south, owing mainly to the predominance of the Hindu religion with its reverence for cows and its ideal of harmonizing the diet with the needs of the soul. Another more practical reason for the widespread uptake is that

egetable growing is a more efficient and economic use of land than aising animals for food.

ulses such as chickpeas and lentils (dhal) are an important source f protein in the vegetarian diet, especially when combined with ther plant protein foods such as rice (as in Kitchiri) or bread. A ypical southern Indian vegetarian meal will usually consist of dhal, wo or three vegetable dishes and a large dish of rice, with some oppadoms, pickles and chutney.

lso to be borne in mind is the fact that meat in India is not always he nutritious and succulent product that we are used to in the west. It s also expensive, and must be heavily supplemented with pulses and egetables to create the necessary balance of nutrients in the diet.

Vegetable Korma

SERVES 4

85 g/3 oz raw cashew nuts
175 ml/6 fl oz boiling water
good pinch of saffron threads, pounded
2 tbsp hot milk
1 small cauliflower, divided into 1-cm/½-inch florets
115 g/4 oz green beans, cut into 2.5-cm/1-inch lengths
115 g/4 oz carrots, cut into 2.5-cm/1-inch sticks
4 tbsp sunflower or olive oil
1 large onion, finely chopped
2 tsp ginger purée
1–2 fresh green chillies, chopped
2 tsp ground coriander
½ tsp ground turmeric
6 tbsp warm water
400 ml/14 fl oz vegetable stock
½ tsp salt, or to taste
250 g/9 oz new potatoes, boiled in their skins, cooled and halved
2 tbsp single cream
2 tsp ghee or butter
1 tsp garam masala
¼ tsp grated nutmeg

1. Soak the cashew nuts in the boiling water in a heatproof bowl for 20 minutes. Meanwhile, soak the pounded saffron in the hot milk.

2. Blanch the vegetables in a saucepan of boiling salted water, then drain and immediately plunge in cold water. The cauliflower and green beans should each be blanched for 3 minutes, while carrots will need 4 minutes.

3. Heat the oil in a medium heavy-based saucepan over a medium heat. Add the onion, ginger purée and chillies and cook, stirring frequently, for 5–6 minutes, until the onion is soft. Add the coriander and turmeric and cook for 1 minute. Add 3 tablespoons of the warm water and cook for 2–3 minutes. Add the remaining warm water, then cook, stirring frequently, for 2–3 minutes, or until the oil separates from the spice paste.

4. Add the stock, saffron and milk mixture and salt, and bring to the boil. Drain the vegetables, add to the saucepan with the potatoes and return to the boil. Reduce the heat to low and simmer for 2–3 minutes.

5. Meanwhile, put the cashew nuts and their soaking water in a food processor and process until well blended. Add to the vegetables, then stir in the cream. Reduce the heat to very low.

6. Melt the ghee in a small saucepan over a low heat. Add the garam masala and nutmeg and sizzle gently for 20–25 seconds. Fold the spiced ghee into the korma. Remove from the heat and serve.

Cumin-scented Aubergine and Potato Curry

SERVES 4

1 large aubergine, about 350 g/12 oz
225 g/8 oz potatoes, boiled in their skins and cooled
3 tbsp sunflower or olive oil
½ tsp black mustard seeds
½ tsp nigella seeds
½ tsp fennel seeds
1 onion, finely chopped
2.5-cm/1-inch piece fresh ginger, grated
2 fresh green chillies, chopped
½ tsp ground cumin
1 tsp ground coriander
1 tsp ground turmeric
½ tsp chilli powder
1 tbsp tomato purée
450 ml/15 fl oz warm water
1 tsp salt, or to taste
½ tsp garam masala
2 tbsp chopped fresh coriander leaves
Indian bread, to serve

1. Quarter the aubergine lengthways and cut the stem end of each quarter into 5-cm/2-inch pieces. Halve the remaining part of each quarter lengthways and cut into the same size as above. Soak the aubergine pieces in cold water.

2. Peel the potatoes and cut into into 5-cm/2-inch cubes. Heat the oil in a large saucepan over a medium heat. When hot, add the mustard seeds and, as soon as they start popping, add the nigella seeds and fennel seeds.

3. Add the onion, ginger and chillies and cook for 7–8 minutes, until the mixture begins to brown.

4. Add the cumin, coriander, turmeric and chilli powder. Cook for about a minute, then add add the tomato purée. Cook for a further minute, pour in the warm water, then add the salt and aubergine. Bring to the boil and cook over a medium heat for 8–10 minutes, stirring frequently to ensure that the aubergine cooks evenly. At the start of cooking, the aubergine will float, but once it soaks up the liquid it will sink quite quickly. As soon as the aubergine sinks, add the potatoes and cook for 2–3 minutes, stirring.

5. Stir in the garam masala and chopped coriander and remove from the heat. Serve with Indian bread.

Green Bean and Potato Curry

SERVES 6

300 ml/10 fl oz vegetable oil
1 tsp white cumin seeds
1 tsp mixed mustard and onion seeds
4 dried red chillies
3 fresh tomatoes, sliced
1 tsp salt
1 tsp fresh ginger, finely chopped
1 tsp crushed fresh garlic
1 tsp chilli powder
200 g/7 oz green beans, diagonally sliced into 2.5-cm/1-inch pieces
2 potatoes, peeled and diced
300 ml/10 fl oz water
chopped fresh coriander and finely sliced green chillies, to garnish

1. Heat the oil in a large, heavy-based saucepan. Add the white cumin seeds, mustard and onion seeds and dried red chillies, stirring well.

2. Add the tomatoes to the pan and stir-fry the mixture for 3–5 minutes.

3. Mix together the salt, ginger, garlic and chilli powder in a bowl and spoon into the saucepan. Blend the whole mixture together.

4. Add the green beans and potatoes to the saucepan and stir-fry for 5 minutes.

5. Add the water to the saucepan, reduce the heat and simmer for 10–15 minutes, stirring occasionally. Transfer to a warmed serving dish, garnish with chopped coriander and green chillies and serve.

Vegetable Sambar

SERVES 6

800 g/1 lb 12 oz canned tomatoes
2 tbsp desiccated coconut
2 tbsp lemon juice
1 tbsp yellow mustard seeds
40 g/1½ oz raw or muscovado sugar
2 tbsp ghee or vegetable oil
2 onions, sliced
4 cardamom pods, lightly crushed
6 curry leaves, plus extra to garnish
2 tsp ground coriander
2 tsp ground cumin
1 tsp ground turmeric
1 tsp ginger purée
200 g/7 oz toor dhal
450 g/1 lb sweet potatoes, cut into chunks
900 g/2 lb potatoes, cut into chunks
2 carrots, sliced
2 courgettes, cut into chunks
1 aubergine, cut into chunks
salt

1. Place the tomatoes and their can juices, the coconut, 1 tablespoon of the lemon juice, the mustard seeds and sugar in a food processor or blender and process until smooth.

2. Heat the ghee in a large, heavy-based saucepan. Add the onion and cook over a low heat, stirring occasionally, for 10 minutes, or until golden. Add the cardamom pods, curry leaves, coriander, cumin, turmeric and ginger purée and cook, stirring constantly, for 1–2 minutes, or until the spices give off their aroma.

3. Stir in the tomato mixture and dhal and bring to the boil. Reduce the heat, cover and simmer for 10 minutes.

4. Add the sweet potatoes, potatoes and carrots, re-cover the saucepan and simmer for a further 15 minutes. Add the courgettes, aubergine and remaining lemon juice, add salt to taste, re-cover and simmer for a further 10–15 minutes, or until the vegetables are tender. Serve garnished with curry leaves.

Spinach and Paneer

SERVES 4

85 g/3 oz ghee or 6 tbsp vegetable or groundnut oil

350 g/12 oz paneer, cut into 1-cm/½-inch pieces

1½ tbsp garlic and ginger purée

1 fresh green chilli, chopped

4 tbsp water

1 onion, finely chopped

600 g/1 lb 5 oz fresh spinach leaves, rinsed and any thick stems removed and rinsed

¼ tsp salt

¼ tsp garam masala

4 tbsp double cream

lemon wedges, to serve

1. Melt the ghee in a flameproof casserole or large frying pan with a tight-fitting lid over a medium–high heat. Add as many paneer pieces as will fit in a single layer without overcrowding the casserole and fry for about 5 minutes until golden brown on all sides. Use a slotted spoon to remove the paneer and drain it on crumpled kitchen paper. Continue, adding a little extra ghee, if necessary, until all the paneer is fried.

2. Put the garlic and ginger purée and chilli in a spice grinder or pestle and mortar and grind until a thick paste forms. Add the water and blend again.

3. Reheat the casserole. Stir in the onion with the garlic and ginger purée mixture and fry, stirring frequently, for 5–8 minutes until the onion is soft, but not brown.

4. Add the spinach, with just the water clinging to the leaves, and the salt, and stir until it wilts. Reduce the heat to low, cover the casserole and continue simmering until the spinach is soft.

5. Stir in the garam masala and cream, then gently return the paneer to the casserole. Simmer, stirring gently, until the paneer is heated through. Taste and adjust the seasoning, if necessary. Serve with lemon wedges for squeezing over.

Okra Stir-fried with Onions

SERVES 4

280 g/10 oz okra
1 small red pepper
1 onion
2 tbsp sunflower or olive oil
1 tsp black or brown mustard seeds
½ tsp cumin seeds
3 large garlic cloves, lightly crushed, then chopped
½ tsp chilli powder
½ tsp salt, or to taste
½ tsp garam masala
freshly cooked basmati rice, to serve

1. Scrub the okra gently, rinse well in cold running water, then slice off the hard head. Halve diagonally and set aside.

2. Remove the seeds and core from the red pepper and cut into 4-cm/1½-inch strips. Halve the onion lengthways and cut into 5-mm/¼-inch thick slices.

3. Heat the oil in a heavy-based frying pan or wok over a medium heat. When hot but not smoking, add the mustard seeds, followed by the cumin seeds. Remove from the heat and add the garlic. Return to a low heat and cook the garlic gently, stirring, for 1 minute, or until lightly browned.

4. Add the okra, red pepper and onion, increase the heat to medium–high and stir-fry for 2 minutes. Add the chilli powder and salt and stir-fry for a further 3 minutes. Add the garam masala and stir-fry for 1 minute. Remove from the heat and serve immediately with freshly cooked basmati rice.

Mushrooms in a Rich Tomato and Onion Sauce

SERVES 4

280 g/10 oz closed cup white mushrooms
4 tbsp sunflower or olive oil
1 onion, finely chopped
1 green chilli, finely chopped
2 tsp garlic purée
1 tsp ground cumin
1 tsp ground coriander
½ tsp chilli powder
½ tsp salt, or to taste
1 tbsp tomato purée
3 tbsp water
1 tbsp snipped fresh chives

1. Wipe the mushrooms with damp kitchen paper and slice thickly.

2. Heat the oil in a medium-sized saucepan over a medium heat. Add the onion and chilli and cook, stirring frequently, for 5–6 minutes, until the onion is soft but not brown. Add the garlic purée and cook, stirring, for 2 minutes.

3. Add the cumin, coriander and chilli powder and cook, stirring, for 1 minute. Add the mushrooms, salt and tomato purée and stir until all the ingredients are thoroughly blended.

4. Sprinkle the water evenly over the mushrooms and reduce the heat to low. Cover and cook for 10 minutes, stirring halfway through. The sauce should have thickened, but if it appears runny, cook, uncovered, for 3–4 minutes, or until you achieve the desired consistency.

5. Transfer to a serving dish, sprinkle with the chives and serve immediately.

Bombay Potatoes

SERVES 6

500 g/1 lb 2 oz new potatoes, diced
1 tsp ground turmeric
4 tbsp ghee or vegetable oil
6 curry leaves
1 dried red chilli
2 fresh green chillies, chopped
½ tsp nigella seeds
1 tsp mixed mustard and onion seeds
½ tsp cumin seeds
½ tsp fennel seeds
¼ tsp asafoetida
2 onions, chopped
5 tbsp chopped fresh coriander
juice of ½ lime
salt

1. Place the potatoes in a large, heavy-based saucepan and pour in just enough cold water to cover. Add ½ teaspoon of the turmeric and a pinch of salt and bring to the boil. Simmer for 10 minutes, or until tender, then drain and reserve until required.

2. Heat the ghee in a large, heavy-based frying pan. Add the curry leaves and dried red chilli and cook, stirring frequently, for a few minutes, or until the chilli is blackened. Add the remaining turmeric, the fresh chillies, the nigella, mustard and onion seeds, cumin and fennel seeds, the asafoetida, onions and fresh coriander and cook, stirring constantly, for 5 minutes, or until the onions have softened.

3. Stir in the potatoes and cook over a low heat, stirring frequently, for 10 minutes, or until heated through. Squeeze over the lime juice and serve.

Potatoes with Spiced Spinach

SERVES 4

350 g/12 oz new potatoes
250 g/9 oz spinach leaves, thawed if frozen
3 tbsp sunflower or olive oil
1 large onion, finely sliced
1 fresh green chilli, finely chopped
2 tsp garlic purée
2 tsp ginger purée
1 tsp ground coriander
½ tsp ground cumin
½ tsp chilli powder
½ tsp ground turmeric
200 g/7 oz canned chopped tomatoes
½ tsp granulated sugar
1 tsp salt, or to taste
3 tbsp single cream

1. Cook the potatoes in their skins in a saucepan of boiling water for 20 minutes, or until tender. Drain, then soak in cold water for 30 minutes. Peel them, if preferred, then halve or quarter.

2. Meanwhile, cook the spinach in a saucepan of boiling water for 2 minutes, then drain. Transfer to a food processor and blend to a purée.

3. Heat 2 tablespoons of the oil in a medium saucepan over a medium heat. Add the onion and cook, stirring, for 10–12 minutes, until browned, reducing the heat to low for the last 2–3 minutes. Remove from the heat and remove the excess oil from the onion by pressing it against the side of the saucepan with a wooden spoon. Drain on kitchen paper.

4. Return the pan to a low heat and add the remaining oil. Add the chilli and garlic and ginger purées and cook over a low heat, stirring, for 2–3 minutes. Add the coriander, cumin, chilli powder and turmeric and cook, stirring, for 1 minute. Add the tomatoes, increase the heat to medium and add the sugar. Cook, stirring, for 5–6 minutes.

5. Add the potatoes, spinach, salt and reserved onion and cook, stirring, for 2–3 minutes. Stir in the cream and cook for 1 minute. Remove from the heat and serve immediately.

Garlic and Chilli-flavoured Potatoes with Cauliflower

SERVES 4

350 g/12 oz new potatoes
1 small cauliflower
2 tbsp sunflower or olive oil
1 tsp black or brown mustard seeds
1 tsp cumin seeds
5 large garlic cloves, lightly crushed, then chopped
1–2 fresh green chillies, finely chopped
½ tsp ground turmeric
½ tsp salt, or to taste
2 tbsp chopped fresh coriander leaves

1. Cook the potatoes in their skins in a saucepan of boiling water for 20 minutes, or until tender. Drain, then soak in cold water for 30 minutes. Peel them, if preferred, then halve or quarter according to their size – the pieces should be only slightly bigger than the size of the cauliflower florets.

2. Meanwhile, divide the cauliflower into about 1-cm/½-inch florets and blanch in a large saucepan of boiling salted water for 3 minutes. Drain and plunge into iced water to prevent further cooking, then drain again.

3. Heat the oil in a medium saucepan over a medium heat. When hot but not smoking, add the mustard seeds, then the cumin seeds. Remove from the heat and add the garlic and chillies. Return to a low heat and cook, stirring, until the garlic has a light brown tinge.

4. Stir in the turmeric, followed by the cauliflower and the potatoes. Add the salt, increase the heat slightly and cook, stirring, until the vegetables are well blended with the spices and heated through.

5. Stir in the coriander, remove from the heat and serve immediately.

Garden Peas and Paneer in Chilli-tomato Sauce

SERVES 4

4 tbsp sunflower or olive oil
250 g/9 oz paneer, cut into 2.5-cm/1-inch cubes
4 green cardamom pods, bruised
2 bay leaves
1 onion, finely chopped
2 tsp garlic purée
2 tsp ginger purée
2 tsp ground coriander
½ tsp ground turmeric
½–1 tsp chilli powder
150 g/5½ oz canned chopped tomatoes
450 ml/16 fl oz warm water
1 tsp salt, or to taste
125 g/4½ oz frozen peas
½ tsp garam masala
2 tbsp single cream
2 tbsp chopped fresh coriander leaves

1. Heat 2 tablespoons of the oil in a medium non-stick saucepan over a medium heat. Add the paneer and cook, stirring frequently, for 3–4 minutes, or until evenly browned. Paneer tends to splatter in hot oil, so be careful. Remove and drain on kitchen paper.

2. Add the remaining oil to the saucepan and reduce the heat to low. Add the cardamom pods and bay leaves and allow to sizzle gently for 20–25 seconds. Add the onion, increase the heat to medium and cook, stirring frequently, for 4–5 minutes, until the onion is soft. Add the garlic and ginger purées and cook, stirring frequently, for a further 3–4 minutes, until the onion is a pale golden colour.

3. Add the ground coriander, turmeric and chilli powder and cook, stirring, for 1 minute. Add the tomatoes and cook, stirring, for 4–5 minutes. Add 2 tablespoons of the warm water and cook, stirring, for 3 minutes, or until the oil separates from the spice paste.

4. Add the remaining warm water and the salt. Bring to the boil, then reduce the heat to low and simmer, uncovered, for 7–8 minutes.

5. Add the paneer and peas and simmer for 5 minutes. Stir in the garam masala, cream and fresh coriander and remove from the heat. Serve immediately.

Chickpeas in Coconut Milk

SERVES 4

275 g/9¾ oz potatoes, cut into 1-cm/½-inch cubes
250 ml/9 fl oz hot water
400 g/14 oz canned chickpeas, drained and well rinsed
250 ml/9 fl oz canned coconut milk
1 tsp salt, or to taste
2 tbsp sunflower or olive oil
4 large garlic cloves, finely chopped or crushed
2 tsp ground coriander
½ tsp ground turmeric
½–1 tsp chilli powder
juice of ½ lemon
Indian bread, to serve

1. Put the potatoes in a medium saucepan and pour in the hot water. Bring to the boil, then reduce the heat to low and cook, covered, for 6–7 minutes. Add the chickpeas and cook, uncovered, for 3–4 minutes, until the potatoes are tender. Add the coconut milk and salt and bring to a slow simmer.

2. Meanwhile, heat the oil in a small saucepan over a low heat. Add the garlic and cook, stirring frequently, until it begins to brown. Add the coriander, turmeric and chilli powder and cook, stirring, for 25–30 seconds.

3. Fold the aromatic oil into the chickpea mixture. Stir in the lemon juice and remove from the heat. Serve immediately with Indian bread.

Tarka Dhal

SERVES 4

200 g/7 oz red split lentils
850 ml/1½ pints water
1 tsp salt, or to taste
2 tsp sunflower or olive oil
½ tsp black or brown mustard seeds
½ tsp cumin seeds
4 shallots, finely chopped
2 green chillies, chopped
1 tsp ground turmeric
1 tsp ground cumin
1 fresh tomato, chopped
2 tbsp chopped fresh coriander leaves
freshly cooked basmati rice or naan, to serve

1. Wash the lentils until the water runs clear and put into a medium-sized saucepan. Add the water and bring to the boil. Reduce the heat to medium and skim off the froth. Cook, uncovered, for 10 minutes. Reduce the heat to low, cover and cook for 45 minutes, stirring occasionally to ensure that the lentils do not stick to the bottom of the pan as they thicken. Stir in the salt.

2. Meanwhile, heat the oil in a small saucepan over a medium heat. When hot but not smoking, add the mustard seeds, followed by the cumin seeds. Add the shallots and chillies and cook, stirring, for 2–3 minutes, then add the turmeric and ground cumin. Add the tomato and cook, stirring, for 30 seconds.

3. Fold the shallot mixture into the cooked lentils. Stir in the coriander, remove from the heat and serve with freshly cooked basmati rice.

Mixed Lentils with Five-spice Seasoning

SERVES 4

- 125 g/4½ oz red split lentils (masoor dhal)
- 125 g/4½ oz skinless split mung beans (mung dhal)
- 900 ml/1½ pints hot water
- 1 tsp ground turmeric
- 1 tsp salt, or to taste
- 1 tbsp lemon juice
- 2 tbsp sunflower or olive oil
- ¼ tsp black mustard seeds
- ¼ tsp cumin seeds
- ¼ tsp nigella seeds
- ¼ tsp fennel seeds
- 4–5 fenugreek seeds
- 2–3 dried red chillies
- 1 small tomato, deseeded and cut into strips, and fresh coriander sprigs, to garnish
- Indian bread, to serve

1. Mix together the lentils and the mung beans and wash until the water runs clear. Put them into a saucepan with the hot water. Bring to the boil and reduce the heat slightly. Let it boil for 5–6 minutes, and when the foam subsides, add the turmeric. Reduce the heat to low, cover and cook for 20 minutes. Add the salt and lemon juice and beat the dhal with a wire beater. Add a little more hot water if the dhal is too thick.

2. Heat the oil in a small saucepan over a medium heat. When hot but not smoking, add the mustard seeds. As soon as they begin to pop, reduce the heat to low and add the cumin, nigella, fennel and fenugreek seeds and the dried chillies. Let the spices sizzle until the seeds begin to pop and the chillies have blackened. Pour the contents of the saucepan over the lentils, scraping off every bit from the saucepan.

3. Turn off the heat and keep the saucepan covered until you are ready to serve. Transfer to a serving dish and garnish with tomato strips and coriander sprigs. Serve as a main course with Indian bread or as an accompaniment to meat, fish or poultry dishes.

Sweet-and-Sour Lentils

SERVES 4

250 g/9 oz split yellow lentils (chana dhal)
1.2 litres/2 pints water
2 bay leaves, torn
3 fresh chillies, sliced once, but left whole
½ tsp ground turmeric
½ tsp asafoetida
3 tbsp vegetable or groundnut oil
½ onion, finely chopped
2-cm/¾-inch piece fresh ginger, finely chopped
30 g/1 oz creamed coconut, grated
1 fresh green chilli, deseeded or not, to taste, and chopped
1½ tbsp sugar
1½ tbsp tamarind paste or tamarind chutney
½ tsp garam masala
¼ tsp ground cumin
¼ tsp ground coriander
salt

TO GARNISH

15 g/½ oz ghee, melted, or 1 tbsp vegetable or groundnut oil
1 tsp garam masala
chopped fresh coriander

1. Put the lentils and water in a large saucepan with a lid over a high heat and bring to the boil, skimming the surface as necessary. When the foam stops rising, stir in the bay leaves, chillies, turmeric and asafoetida. Half-cover the pan and leave the lentils to continue simmering for about 40 minutes, or until they are very tender, but not reduced to a mush, and all the liquid has been absorbed.

2. When the lentils are almost tender, heat the oil in a kadhai, wok or large frying pan over a medium-high heat. Add the onion and ginger and fry, stirring frequently, for 5–8 minutes.

3. Stir in the coconut, green chilli, sugar, tamarind paste, garam masala, cumin and ground coriander and stir for about 1 minute.

4. When the lentils are tender, add them to the spice mixture with the bay leaves, chillies and any liquid left in the saucepan, and stir around to blend together. Taste and add salt, if necessary, and extra sugar and tamarind, if desired.

5. Transfer the lentils to a serving dish and drizzle the hot ghee over the top. Sprinkle with garam masala and coriander and serve immediately

Kitchri

SERVES 4–6

225 g/8 oz basmati rice
30 g/1 oz ghee or 2 tbsp vegetable or groundnut oil
1 large onion, finely chopped
250 g/9 oz red split lentils (masoor dhal), rinsed
2 tsp garam masala
1½ tsp salt, or to taste
pinch of asafoetida
850 ml/1½ pints water
2 tbsp chopped fresh coriander
chapattis and raita, to serve

1. Rinse the basmati rice in several changes of water until the water runs clear, then leave to soak for 30 minutes. Drain and set aside until ready to cook.

2. Melt the ghee in a flameproof casserole or large saucepan with a tight-fitting lid over a medium–high heat. Add the onion and fry for 5–8 minutes, stirring frequently, until golden, but not brown.

3. Stir in the rice and lentils along with the garam masala, salt and asafoetida, and stir for 2 minutes. Pour in the water and bring to the boil, stirring.

4. Reduce the heat to low and cover the pan tightly. Simmer without lifting the lid for 20 minutes, until the grains are tender and the liquid is absorbed. Re-cover the pan, turn off the heat and leave to stand for 5 minutes.

5. Use 2 forks to mix in the coriander and adjust the seasoning, adding more salt if necessary. Serve with chapattis and raita.

Snacks and Accompaniments

Indians love to eat all kinds of appetizing snacks, especially before the main meal or to nibble on with drinks. Snack foods range from simple sweet and spicy nuts or plantain chips to deep-fried onion bhajis, crispy vegetable samosa triangles and sweet and spicy nuts.

Also important on the Indian culinary map are the numerous breads and rice dishes that are standard accompaniments to a typical Indian meal. Breads are essential for mopping up sauces and for making meals easier to eat with the hand. They are usually unleavened and are quick and easy to make as very little kneading and rising time is needed. Bread appears in many forms – deep-fried pooris and crispy poppadoms, oven-baked naan, griddled chapattis and parathas – all are equally delicious.

A bowl of steamed or boiled fluffy rice, delicately flavoured with mild spices or coconut, is usually served with the main meal, although bread is preferred in the north. Sometimes the rice is baked in a pulao with flavoursome stock instead of water. Pulaos are lightly spiced and always include plenty of butter and tasty garnishes such as almonds, fried onions, sultanas or raisins.

No Indian meal would be complete without a tray of chutneys, freshly made pickles and cooling sauces such as cucumber in spiced yogurt or tomato kachumbar. Not only are these served as traditional accompaniments to meat and fish dishes, but, in a land where vegetarianism is a way of life for many, they are an important supplement to meat-free meals.

Sweet and Spicy Nuts

SERVES 6–8

300 g/10½ oz caster sugar

1 tsp sea salt

2 tbsp mild, medium or hot curry powder, to taste

1 tsp ground turmeric

1 tsp ground coriander

pinch of chilli powder

450 g/1 lb mixed whole blanched almonds and shelled cashew nuts

vegetable or groundnut oil, for deep-frying

1. Mix together the sugar, salt, curry powder, turmeric, coriander and chilli powder in a large bowl, then set aside.

2. Meanwhile, bring a large saucepan of water to the boil. Add the almonds and cashews and blanch for 1 minute, then tip them into a sieve to drain, and shake off as much of the excess water as possible. Immediately toss the nuts with the sugar and spices.

3. Heat enough oil for deep-frying in a wok, deep-fat fryer or large heavy-based saucepan to 180°C/350°F, or until a cube of bread browns in 30 seconds. Use a slotted spoon to remove the nuts from the spice mixture, leaving the spice mixture behind in the bowl, then drop the nuts into the hot oil. Fry them for 3–4 minutes, stirring occasionally and watching carefully because they can burn quickly, until they turn golden.

4. Remove the nuts from the oil with the slotted spoon and toss them in the remaining spice mixture. Tip the nuts into a sieve and shake off the excess spices, then leave to cool completely and crisp up. Store in an airtight container for up to a week.

Bhel Poori

SERVES 4

300 g/10½ oz new potatoes
200 g/7 oz canned chickpeas, rinsed and very well drained
100 g/3½ oz sev noodles
55 g/2 oz puffed rice
4 tbsp raisins
2 tbsp chopped fresh coriander
1 tbsp fennel seeds, toasted and cooled
pooris, crushed
salt

CHAAT MASALA
1 tbsp coriander seeds
1 tbsp cumin seeds
1 tsp black peppercorns
2 dried red chillies

TO SERVE
natural yogurt
tamarind chutney
coriander chutney

1. Bring a large saucepan of salted water to the boil and cook the potatoes for 12–15 minutes, until tender. Drain and run under cold water to cool, then peel and cut into 5-mm/¼-inch dice. Cover and chill for at least 30 minutes.

2. Meanwhile, to make the chaat masala, heat a dry frying pan over a high heat. Add the coriander and cumin seeds, peppercorns and chillies and stir around until they give off their aroma, watching closely because the cumin seeds burn quickly. Immediately tip them out of the pan to stop the cooking. Grind the toasted spice mixture in a spice grinder or with a pestle and mortar.

3. Use your hands to toss together the potatoes, chickpeas, sev noodles, puffed rice, raisins, coriander, fennel seeds and crushed pooris. Sprinkle with the chaat masala and toss again.

4. Divide the mixture between small serving bowls or place in one large bowl and drizzle to taste with the yogurt and chutneys. It is best eaten straight away so that it doesn't become soggy.

Plantain Chips

SERVES 4

4 ripe plantains

1 tsp mild, medium or hot curry powder, to taste

vegetable or groundnut oil, for deep-frying

mango chutney, to serve

1. Peel the plantains, then cut crossways into 3-mm/1⁄8-inch slices. Put the slices in a bowl, sprinkle over the curry powder and use your hands to toss lightly together.

2. Heat enough oil for deep-frying in a wok, deep-fat fryer or large heavy-based saucepan to 180°C/350°F, or until a cube of bread browns in 30 seconds. Add as many plantain slices as will fit in the pan without overcrowding and fry for 2 minutes, or until golden.

3. Remove the plantain chips from the pan with a slotted spoon and drain well on crumpled kitchen paper. Serve hot with mango chutney.

Onion Bhajis

SERVES 4

150 g/5½ oz gram flour
1 tsp salt, or to taste
small pinch of bicarbonate of soda
25 g/1 oz ground rice
1 tsp fennel seeds
1 tsp cumin seeds
2 green chillies, finely chopped
2 large onions, about 400 g/14 oz, sliced into half-rings and separated
15 g/½ oz fresh coriander, including the tender stalks, finely chopped
200 ml/7 fl oz water
sunflower or olive oil, for deep-frying
tomato or mango chutney, to serve

1. Sift the gram flour into a large bowl and add the salt, bicarbonate of soda, ground rice and fennel and cumin seeds. Mix together thoroughly, then add the chillies, onions and coriander. Gradually pour in the water and mix until a thick batter is formed and all the other ingredients are thoroughly coated with it.

2. Heat enough oil for deep-frying in a wok, deep saucepan or deep-fat fryer to 180°C/350°F, or until a cube of bread browns in 30 seconds. If the oil is not hot enough, the bhajis will be soggy. Add as many ½ tablespoons of the batter as will fit in a single layer, without overcrowding. Reduce the heat slightly and cook the bhajis for 8–10 minutes, until golden brown and crisp. Maintaining a steady temperature is important to ensure that the centres of the bhajis are cooked, while the outsides turn brown. Remove and drain on kitchen paper. Keep hot in a low oven while you cook the remaining batter.

3. Serve hot with a tomato or mango chutney.

Vegetable Samosas

MAKES 12

3 tbsp sunflower or olive oil
½ tsp black mustard seeds
1 tsp cumin seeds
1 tsp fennel seeds
1 onion, finely chopped
2 green chillies, finely chopped
2 tsp ginger purée
½ tsp ground turmeric
1 tsp ground coriander
1 tsp ground cumin
½ tsp chilli powder
350 g/12 oz boiled potatoes, cut into bite-sized pieces
125 g/4½ oz frozen peas, thawed
1 tsp salt, or to taste
2 tbsp chopped fresh coriander leaves
12 sheets filo pastry, about 28 x 18 cm/11 x 7 inches
55 g/2 oz butter, melted, plus extra for greasing
chutney, to serve

1. Heat the oil in a saucepan over a medium heat and add the mustard seeds, followed by the cumin and fennel seeds. Then add the onion, chillies and ginger purée and cook, stirring frequently, for 5–6 minutes, until the onion is soft but not brown.

2. Add the ground spices and cook, stirring, for 1 minute. Add the potatoes, peas and salt and stir until the vegetables are thoroughly coated with the spices. Stir in the coriander and remove from the heat. Leave to cool completely.

3. Preheat the oven to 180°C/350°F/Gas Mark 4 and line a baking sheet with greased greaseproof paper or baking paper.

4. Place a sheet of filo pastry on a board and brush well with the melted butter. Keep the remaining pastry sheets covered with a moist cloth or clingfilm. Fold the buttered pastry sheet in half lengthways, brush with some more melted butter and fold lengthways again.

5. Place about 1 tablespoon of the vegetable filling on the bottom right-hand corner of the pastry sheet and fold over to form a triangle. Continue folding to the top of the sheet, maintaining the triangular shape, and moisten the ends to seal the edges. Transfer to the prepared baking sheet and brush with melted butter. Repeat with the remaining sheets of filo pastry and filling.

6. Bake the samosas in the preheated oven on a shelf just below the top rung of the oven for 20 minutes, or until browned. Serve hot with chutney.

Spicy Pancakes

SERVES 6

- 140 g/5 oz basmati rice, soaked for 2–3 hours in cold water and drained
- 140 g/5 oz black lentils, soaked for 2–3 hours in cold water and drained
- 2 fresh green chillies, deseeded and finely chopped
- 1 tsp dark brown sugar
- 300 ml/10 fl oz water
- 1.25 kg/2 lb 12 oz potatoes
- 3 tbsp grated fresh coconut
- 2.5-cm/1-inch piece fresh ginger, finely chopped
- 4 tbsp ghee or vegetable oil, plus extra for frying
- 2 tsp black mustard seeds
- 2 tsp cumin seeds
- 1 tsp ground turmeric
- 3 tbsp chopped fresh coriander
- salt
- fresh mint sprigs, to garnish
- chutney, to serve

1. Place the rice and black lentils in a food processor and process until ground. Tip into a bowl. Stir in half the chillies, the sugar and a pinch of salt. Gradually add the water and mix to a smooth batter. Cover and leave to stand in a warm place overnight.

2. Cook the potatoes in lightly salted boiling water for 20–25 minutes, or until tender. Drain and mash. Mix the remaining chillies, coconut and ginger to a paste.

3. Heat the ghee in a large, heavy-based frying pan, add the mustard and cumin seeds and stir until they give off their aroma. Stir in the coconut and ginger paste and cook for 1 minute, then add the mashed potatoes, turmeric and coriander and cook, stirring, for 5 minutes. Remove from the heat.

4. Heat a little ghee in a 20-cm/8-inch frying pan. Stir the batter. Pour one-sixth into the frying pan, tilting the pan to spread it over the base. Cook for 1–2 minutes, or until the underside is golden. Flip over and cook the other side for 2 minutes. Transfer to a plate and keep warm while you cook the remaining pancakes, adding more ghee as required. Divide the filling between the pancakes and fold in half. Return them to the frying pan, in batches, and fry for 30 seconds on each side. Garnish with fresh mint sprigs and serve with chutney.

Deep-fried Potato Balls

SERVES 4

450 g/1 lb potatoes, boiled and diced
1 onion, chopped
2.5-cm/1-inch piece fresh ginger, finely chopped
1 fresh green chilli, deseeded and finely chopped
1 tbsp chopped fresh coriander
1 tbsp lemon juice
2 tsp aamchoor (dried mango powder)
vegetable oil, for deep-frying
salt
chutney, to serve

BATTER
115 g/4 oz gram flour
¼ tsp baking powder
¼ tsp chilli powder
about 150 ml/5 fl oz water
salt

1. To make the batter, sift the flour, baking powder, chilli powder and a pinch of salt into a bowl. Gradually, stir in enough cold water to make a smooth batter. Cover with clingfilm and reserve.

2. Place the potatoes, onion, ginger, chilli, coriander, lemon juice and amchoor in a separate bowl. Mix together well with a wooden spoon, breaking up the potatoes. Season with salt to taste. Break off small pieces of the mixture and form into balls between the palms of your hands.

3. Heat enough oil for deep-frying in a wok, deep-fat fryer or large heavy-based saucepan to 180°C/350°F, or until a cube of bread browns in 30 seconds. When the oil is hot, dip the potato balls in the batter, using a fork, and add to the oil, in batches. Deep-fry for 3–4 minutes, until golden brown. Remove with a slotted spoon and drain on kitchen paper. Keep each batch warm while you cook the remainder. Serve hot, with chutney.

Chilli-coriander Naan

SERVES 8

450 g/1 lb plain flour
2 tsp sugar
1 tsp salt
1 tsp baking powder
1 egg
250 ml/9 fl oz milk
2 tbsp sunflower or olive oil, plus extra for oiling
2 fresh red chillies, chopped
15 g/½ oz fresh coriander leaves, chopped
2 tbsp butter, melted

1. Sift together the flour, sugar, salt and baking powder into a large bowl. Whisk together the egg and milk and gradually add to the flour mixture, mixing with a wooden spoon until a dough is formed.

2. Transfer the dough to a work surface, make a depression in the centre of the dough and add the oil. Knead for 3–4 minutes, until the oil is absorbed by the flour and you have a smooth and pliable dough. Wrap the dough in clingfilm and leave to rest for 1 hour.

3. Divide the dough into 8 equal-sized pieces, form each piece into a ball and flatten into a thick cake. Cover the dough cakes with clingfilm and leave to rest for 10–15 minutes.

4. Preheat the grill to high. Line a grill pan with a piece of foil and brush with oil.

5. The traditional shape of naan is teardrop, but you can make them any shape you wish. To make the traditional shape, roll each flattened cake into a 13-cm/5-inch round and pull the lower end gently. Carefully roll out again, maintaining the teardrop shape, to about 23 cm/9 inches in diameter. Alternatively, roll the flattened cakes out to 23-cm/9-inch rounds.

6. Mix the chillies and coriander together, then divide into 8 equal portions and spread each on the surface of a naan. Press gently so that the mixture sticks to the dough. Transfer a naan to the prepared grill pan and cook 13 cm/5 inches below the heat source for 1 minute, or until slightly puffed and brown patches appear on the surface. Watch carefully, and as soon as brown spots appear on the surface, turn over and cook the other side for 45–50 seconds, until lightly browned. Remove from the grill and brush with the melted butter. Wrap in a tea towel while you cook the remaining naans.

Chapattis

MAKES 16

400 g/14 oz chapatti flour (atta), plus extra for dusting
1 tsp salt
½ tsp granulated sugar
2 tbsp sunflower or olive oil
250 ml/9 fl oz lukewarm water

1. Mix together the chapatti flour, salt and sugar in a large bowl. Add the oil and work well into the flour mixture with your fingertips. Gradually add the water, mixing at the same time. When the dough is formed, transfer to a work surface and knead for 4–5 minutes. The dough is ready when all the excess moisture is absorbed by the flour. Alternatively, mix the dough in a food processor. Wrap the dough in clingfilm and leave to rest for 30 minutes.

2. Divide the dough in half, then cut each half into 8 equal-sized pieces. Form each piece into a ball and flatten into a round cake. Lightly dust each cake in the flour and roll out to a 15-cm/6-inch round. Keep the remaining cakes covered while you are working on one. The chapattis will cook better when freshly rolled out, so roll out and cook one at a time.

3. Preheat a heavy-based cast-iron griddle or a large heavy-based frying pan over a medium–high heat. Put a chapatti on the griddle and cook for 30 seconds. Using a fish slice, turn over and cook until bubbles begin to appear on the surface. Turn over again. Gently press the edges down with a clean cloth to encourage the chapatti to puff up – they will not always puff up, but this doesn't matter. Cook until brown patches appear on the underside. Remove from the pan and keep hot by wrapping in a piece of foil lined with kitchen paper. Repeat with the remaining chapattis.

Pooris

MAKES 12

225 g/8 oz wholemeal flour, sifted, plus extra for dusting

½ teaspoon salt

30 g/1 oz ghee, melted

100–150 ml/3½–5 fl oz water

vegetable or groundnut oil, for deep-frying

1. Put the flour and salt into a bowl and drizzle the ghee over the surface. Gradually stir in the water until a stiff dough forms.

2. Turn out the dough onto a lightly floured surface and knead for 10 minutes, or until it is smooth and elastic. Shape the dough into a ball and place it in the cleaned bowl, then cover with a damp tea towel and leave to rest for 20 minutes.

3. Divide the dough into 12 equal-sized pieces and roll each into a ball. Working with one ball of dough at a time, flatten the dough between your palms, then thinly roll it out on a lightly floured work surface into a 13-cm/5-inch round. Continue until all the dough balls are rolled out.

4. Heat enough oil for deep-frying in a wok, deep-fat fryer or large heavy-based saucepan to 180°C/350°F, or until a cube of bread browns in 30 seconds. Drop one poori into the hot fat and fry for about 10 seconds, or until it puffs up.

5. Use the 2 spoons to lift the poori from the oil and let any excess oil drip back into the pan. Drain the poori on crumpled kitchen paper and serve immediately. Continue until all the pooris are fried, making sure the oil returns to the correct temperature before you add another poori.

Pilau Rice

SERVES 2–4

200 g/7 oz basmati rice
2 tbsp ghee
3 green cardamoms
2 whole cloves
3 black peppercorns
½ tsp salt
½ tsp saffron threads
400 ml/14 fl oz water

1. Rinse the basmati rice in several changes of water until the water runs clear, then leave to soak for 30 minutes. Drain and set aside until ready to cook.

2. Heat the ghee in a large, heavy-based saucepan. Add the cardamoms, cloves and peppercorns and fry, stirring, for 1 minute. Add the rice and stir-fry for a further 2 minutes.

3. Add the salt, saffron and water to the rice mixture and reduce the heat. Cover the saucepan and leave to simmer over a low heat for 20 minutes, until all the water has evaporated.

4. Transfer the rice to a large, warmed serving dish and serve hot.

Coconut Rice

SERVES 4–6

225 g/8 oz basmati rice
450 ml/16 fl oz water
60 g/2¼ oz creamed coconut
2 tbsp mustard oil
1½ tsp salt

1. Rinse the basmati rice in several changes of water until the water runs clear, then leave to soak for 30 minutes. Drain and set aside until ready to cook.

2. Bring the water to the boil in a small saucepan, stir in the creamed coconut until it dissolves and then set aside.

3. Heat the mustard oil in a large frying pan or saucepan with a lid over a high heat until it smokes. Turn off the heat and leave the mustard oil to cool completely.

4. When you are ready to cook, reheat the mustard oil over a medium–high heat. Add the rice and stir until all the grains are coated in oil. Add the water with the dissolved coconut and bring to the boil.

5. Reduce the heat to its lowest setting, stir in the salt and cover the pan tightly. Simmer, without lifting the lid, for 8–10 minutes, until the grains are tender and all the liquid is absorbed.

6. Turn off the heat and use 2 forks to mix the rice. Adjust the seasoning, if necessary. Re-cover the pan and leave the rice to stand for 5 minutes.

Raita

SERVES 4–5

1 small cucumber
175 g/6 oz whole milk natural yogurt
¼ tsp granulated sugar
¼ tsp salt
1 tsp cumin seeds
10–12 black peppercorns
¼ tsp paprika

1. Peel the cucumber and scoop out the seeds. Cut the flesh into bite-sized pieces and set aside.

2. Put the yogurt in a bowl and beat with a fork until smooth. Add the sugar and salt and mix well.

3. Preheat a small, heavy-based saucepan over a medium–high heat. When the pan is hot, turn off the heat and add the cumin seeds and peppercorns. Stir around for 40–50 seconds, until they release their aroma. Remove from the pan and leave to cool for 5 minutes, then crush in a mortar with a pestle or on a hard surface with a rolling pin. Reserve ¼ teaspoon of this mixture and stir the remainder into the yogurt. Add the cucumber and stir to mix.

4. Transfer the raita to a serving dish and sprinkle with the reserved toasted spices and the paprika.

Tomato Kachumbar

SERVES 6

125 ml/4 fl oz lime juice
½ tsp sugar
6 tomatoes, chopped
½ cucumber, chopped
8 spring onions, chopped
1 fresh green chilli, deseeded and chopped
1 tbsp chopped fresh coriander
1 tbsp chopped fresh mint
salt

1. Mix the lime juice, sugar and a pinch of salt together in a large bowl and stir until the sugar has completely dissolved.

2. Add the tomatoes, cucumber, spring onions, chilli, coriander and mint and toss well to mix.

3. Cover with clingfilm and leave to chill in the refrigerator for at least 30 minutes. Toss the vegetables before serving.

Coriander Chutney

SERVES 4–5

1½ tbsp lemon juice
1½ tbsp water
85 g/3 oz fresh coriander leaves and stems, roughly chopped
2 tbsp chopped fresh coconut
1 small shallot, very finely chopped
5-mm/¼-inch piece fresh ginger, chopped
1 fresh green chilli, deseeded and chopped
½ tsp sugar
½ tsp salt
pinch of pepper

1. Put the lemon juice and water in a small food processor, add half the coriander and whizz until it is blended and a slushy paste forms. Gradually add the remaining coriander and whizz until it is all blended, scraping down the sides of the processor, if necessary.

2. If you don't have a processor that will cope with this small amount, use a pestle and mortar, adding the coriander in small amounts.

3. Add the remaining ingredients and continue processing until they are all finely chopped and blended. Taste and adjust the seasonings, if necessary. Transfer to a non-metallic bowl, cover and chill for up to 3 days before serving.

Mango Chutney

SERVES 4–6

- 1 large mango, about 400 g/14 oz, peeled, stoned and finely chopped
- 2 tbsp lime juice
- 1 tbsp vegetable or groundnut oil
- 2 shallots, finely chopped
- 1 garlic clove, finely chopped
- 2 fresh green chillies, deseeded and finely sliced
- 1 tsp black mustard seeds
- 1 tsp coriander seeds
- 5 tbsp palm sugar or soft light brown sugar
- 5 tbsp white wine vinegar
- 1 tsp salt
- pinch of ground ginger

1. Put the mango in a non-metallic bowl with the lime juice and set aside.

2. Heat the oil in a large frying pan or saucepan over a medium–high heat. Add the shallots and cook for 3 minutes. Add the garlic and chillies and stir for a further 2 minutes, or until the shallots are soft but not brown. Add the mustard seeds and coriander seeds and stir around.

3. Add the mango to the pan with the palm sugar, vinegar, salt and ground ginger and stir around. Reduce the heat to its lowest setting and simmer for 10 minutes, until the liquid thickens and the mango becomes sticky.

4. Remove from the heat and leave to cool completely. Transfer to an airtight container, cover and chill for 3 days before using.

Lime Pickle

SERVES 6–8

12 limes, halved and deseeded
115 g/4 oz salt
70 g/2½ oz chilli powder
25 g/1 oz mustard powder
25 g/1 oz ground fenugreek
1 tbsp ground turmeric
300 ml/10 fl oz mustard oil
15 g/½ oz yellow mustard seeds, crushed
½ tsp asafoetida

1. Cut each lime half into 4 pieces and pack them into a large sterilized jar, sprinkling over the salt at the same time. Cover and leave to stand in a warm place for 10–14 days, or until the limes have turned brown and softened.

2. Mix together the chilli powder, mustard powder, fenugreek and turmeric in a small bowl and add to the jar of limes. Stir to mix, then re-cover and leave to stand for 2 days.

3. Transfer the lime mixture to a heatproof bowl. Heat the mustard oil in a heavy-based frying pan. Add the mustard seeds and asafoetida to the pan and cook, stirring constantly, until the oil is very hot and just beginning to smoke.

4. Pour the oil and spices over the limes and mix well. Cover and leave to cool. When cool, pack into a sterilized jar, seal and store in a sunny place for 1 week before serving.

Desserts and Drinks

Indian meals traditionally finish with a selection of plain fresh fruit such as mangoes, guavas, pineapples or melons, always carefully sliced and beautifully presented. Fruit is generally served chilled, especially in the summer months, and makes a delicious contrast to the warm, spicy main course.

Another much appreciated cooling dessert is kulfi – a type of Indian ice cream frozen in special cone-shape moulds and traditionally made by long-boiling milk until it is reduced to a thick, golden and richly flavoured cream. However, it is also more quickly and easily made with evaporated milk. Kulfi may be served plain but is often flavoured with saffron, mango or coconut. It is delicious sprinkled with chopped pistachios or almonds.

On special occasions such as birthday, wedding or religious feasts, a very rich sweet dessert is served. This might be sweet saffron rice with

caramelized pineapple, or creamy shrikhand made with spiced and sweetened yogurt 'cheese', garnished with jewel-like pomegranate seeds. Indians love sweetmeats such as sweet carrot halva, which are eaten as snacks at any time of day.

With India's sky-high temperatures, there is no shortage of refreshing non-alcoholic drinks – spicy fruit cordials and juices, chilled mineral or soda water flavoured with ginger or lime and black pepper, or even hot milky tea served in small glasses, sometimes made fragrant with cardamom and other sweet spices. Also popular is lassi, a chilled lightly spiced drink made with whisked yogurt diluted with water. Lassi may be sweet or salty and is served throughout India but particularly in the north where it is popular at breakfast.

Saffron and Almond Kulfi

MAKES 4

½ tsp saffron threads
75 ml/2½ fl oz milk
1 tbsp ground rice
½ tbsp ground almonds
225 ml/8 fl oz canned evaporated milk
225 ml/8 fl oz double cream
2 tbsp caster sugar
2 tbsp chopped toasted blanched almonds, to serve

1. Put the saffron threads in a dry frying pan over a high heat and 'toast', stirring frequently until you can smell the aroma, then immediately tip them out of the pan and reserve.

2. Put the milk in the frying pan over a medium–high heat, add the saffron threads and heat just until small bubbles appear around the edge. Remove the pan from the heat and leave the saffron to infuse for at least 15 minutes. Meanwhile, combine the ground rice and ground almonds in a heatproof bowl. Put a shallow freezerproof container into the freezer.

3. Reheat the milk and saffron just until small bubbles appear around the edge, then slowly beat the milk into the almond mixture, beating until it is smooth without any lumps. Pour the evaporated milk into a pan over a medium–high heat and bring to the boil, stirring. Remove the pan from the heat and stir into the milk mixture. Stir in the cream and sugar.

4. Return the pan to a medium heat and simmer, stirring constantly, for 5–10 minutes until the mixture thickens, but do not boil. Remove the pan from the heat and set aside to cool, stirring frequently.

5. Pour the saffron mixture into the freezerproof container and freeze for 30 minutes, then beat to break up any ice crystals. Continue beating every 30 minutes until the ice cream is thick and almost firm. If you are using metal kulfi moulds, put them in the freezer now.

6. Divide the mixture equally between 4 kulfi moulds or ramekins. Cover with lids or clingfilm and freeze for at least 2 hours until solid.

7. To serve, dip a cloth in hot water, wring it out and rub it around the sides of the moulds or ramekins, then invert onto plates. Sprinkle with the toasted almonds and serve.

Carrot Halva

SERVES 4–6

55 g/2 oz ghee or unsalted butter
2.5-cm/1-inch piece cinnamon stick, halved
25 g/1 oz flaked almonds
25 g/1 oz cashew nuts
25 g /1 oz seedless raisins
450 g/1 lb grated carrots
600 ml/1 pint milk
125 g/4½ oz caster sugar
½ tsp freshly ground cardamom seeds
½ tsp freshly grated nutmeg
50 ml/2 fl oz double cream
2 tbsp rosewater
vanilla ice cream or whipped double cream, to serve

1. Melt the ghee in a heavy-based saucepan over a low heat. Add the cinnamon stick and leave to sizzle gently for 25–30 seconds. Add the almonds and cashew nuts and cook, stirring, until lightly browned. Remove about a dessertspoon of the nuts and reserve.

2. Add the raisins, carrots, milk and sugar to the saucepan, increase the heat to medium and bring the milk to boiling point. Continue to cook over a low–medium heat for 15–20 minutes, until the milk evaporates completely, stirring frequently, and scraping and blending in any thickened milk that sticks to the side of the saucepan. Don't allow any milk that is stuck to the side to brown or burn, as this will give the dessert an unpleasant flavour.

3. Stir in the cardamom, nutmeg, cream and rosewater. Remove from the heat and leave to cool slightly, then serve topped with a scoop of vanilla ice cream or whipped double cream. Sprinkle over the reserved nuts to decorate.

Sweet Saffron Rice with Caramelized Pineapple

SERVES 4–6

good pinch of saffron threads, pounded
2 tbsp hot milk
175 g/6 oz basmati rice
½ fresh pineapple (225 g/8 oz prepared weight)
55 g/2 oz ghee or unsalted butter
150–175 g/5½–6 oz caster sugar
4 green cardamom pods, bruised
4 cloves
2 x 1-cm/½-inch pieces cinnamon stick
300 ml/10 fl oz warm water
melted butter or vegetable oil, for brushing
55 g/2 oz seedless raisins
25 g/1 oz toasted flaked almonds, to decorate
single cream, to serve

1. Preheat the oven to 160°C/325°F/Gas Mark 3. Soak the pounded saffron in the hot milk. Wash the rice in several changes of cold water, then leave to drain in a colander.

2. Peel the pineapple and remove the 'eyes' with a small, sharp knife. Cut the flesh into bite-sized pieces. Melt 1 tablespoon of the ghee in a large, heavy-based frying pan over a low heat. Add the pineapple, sprinkle with 2 tablespoons of the sugar and increase the heat to high. Cook, stirring, for 3–4 minutes, or until the pineapple begins to caramelize a little, then remove from the heat.

3. Melt the remaining ghee in a heavy-based saucepan over a low heat. Add the cardamom pods, cloves and cinnamon stick and cook, stirring, for 25–30 seconds. Add the rice, increase the heat slightly and cook, stirring, for 2–3 minutes. Add the saffron and milk and the warm water, bring to the boil and boil for 2 minutes, then reduce the heat to low. Cook, uncovered, for 2–3 minutes, until the surface liquid has been absorbed by the grains. Remove from the heat.

4. Brush the sides and the base of a lidded ovenproof dish with a little butter and add one-third of the rice. Top with one-third of the raisins, followed by one third of the pineapple pieces. Sprinkle over one-third of the remaining sugar evenly. Repeat this process twice more, ensuring that you finish with a layer of raisins, pineapple and sugar.

5. Soak a piece of greaseproof paper, crumple it, then place loosely over the top layer of fruit and sugar. Cover with a piece of foil and seal the edges by pressing it round the entire rim. Put the lid on and bake in the centre of the preheated oven for 35–40 minutes. Turn off the oven and leave the rice to stand in the oven for 10–15 minutes.

6. The dessert can be served hot or cold. Decorate with the flaked almonds and serve with cream.

Indian Rice Dessert

SERVES 4

good pinch of saffron threads, pounded
2 tbsp hot milk
40 g/1½ oz ghee or unsalted butter
55 g/2 oz ground rice
25 g/1 oz flaked almonds
25 g/1 oz seedless raisins
600 ml/1 pint milk
450 ml/16 fl oz evaporated milk
55 g/2 oz caster sugar
12 ready-to-eat dried apricots, sliced
1 tsp freshly ground cardamom seeds
½ tsp freshly grated nutmeg
2 tbsp rosewater

TO DECORATE

25 g/1 oz walnut pieces
15 g/½ oz shelled unsalted pistachio nuts

1. Place the pounded saffron in the hot milk and leave to soak until needed.

2. Reserve 2 teaspoons of the ghee and melt the remainder in a heavy-based saucepan over a low heat. Add the ground rice, almonds and raisins and cook, stirring, for 2 minutes. Add the milk, increase the heat to medium and cook, stirring, until it begins to bubble gently. Reduce the heat to low and cook for 10–12 minutes, stirring frequently, to prevent the mixture sticking to the bottom of the pan.

3. Add the evaporated milk, sugar and apricots, reserving a few slices to decorate. Cook, stirring, until the mixture thickens to the consistency of a pouring custard.

4. Add the cardamom, nutmeg and rosewater, stir to distribute well and remove from the heat. Leave to cool, then cover and chill in the refrigerator for at least 2 hours.

5. Melt the reserved ghee in a small saucepan over a low heat. Add the walnuts and cook, stirring, until they brown a little. Remove and drain on kitchen paper. Brown the pistachio nuts in the remaining ghee in the saucepan, then remove and drain on kitchen paper. Leave the pistachio nuts to cool, then lightly crush.

6. Serve the dessert decorated with the fried nuts and the reserved apricot slices.

Shrikhand with Pomegranate

SERVES 4–6

1 litre/1¾ pints natural yogurt
¼ tsp saffron threads
2 tbsp milk
55 g/2 oz caster sugar, or to taste
seeds from 2 green cardamom pods
2 pomegranates, or other exotic fruit

1. Line a sieve set over a bowl with a piece of muslin large enough to hang over the edge. Add the yogurt, then tie the corners of the muslin into a tight knot. Tie the bundle to a tap and leave to hang over the sink for 4 hours, or until all the excess moisture drips away.

2. Put the saffron threads in a dry saucepan over a high heat and 'toast', stirring frequently, until you can smell the aroma. Immediately tip them out of the pan and reserve. Put the milk in the pan, return the saffron threads and warm the milk just until bubbles appear around the edge, then set aside and leave to infuse.

3. When the yogurt is thick and creamy, put it in a bowl and stir in the sugar, cardamom seeds and saffron mixture and beat until smooth. Taste and add extra sugar, if desired. Cover and chill for at least 1 hour, until well chilled.

4. Meanwhile, to prepare the pomegranate seeds, cut the fruit in half and use a small teaspoon or your fingers to scoop out the seeds.

5. To serve, spoon the yogurt into individual bowls or plates and add the pomegranate seeds.

Ginger Ice Cream with Date and Tamarind Sauce

SERVES 4–5

ICE CREAM

1-litre/1¾-pint carton vanilla ice cream

2 tsp ground ginger

200 g/7 oz chopped crystallized ginger, to serve

TAMARIND SAUCE

55 g/2 oz seedless raisins

85 g/3 oz stoned dried dates

250 ml/9 fl oz boiling water

2 rounded tsp tamarind concentrate or 3 tbsp tamarind juice

25 g/1 oz molasses sugar

1. Leave the ice cream at room temperature for 35–40 minutes to soften, then transfer to a bowl. Add the ground ginger and beat well. Return to the carton and freeze for 3–4 hours.

2. Meanwhile, to make the sauce, put the raisins and dates in a heatproof bowl, pour over the boiling water and leave to soak for 15–20 minutes. Transfer to a blender or food processor, add the tamarind and sugar and blend to a smooth purée. Transfer to a non-metallic bowl and leave to cool.

3. Put scoops of the ice cream into serving dishes and drizzle over the sauce. Arrange about 1 dessertspoon of crystallized ginger on top of each dessert and serve immediately. Serve any extra sauce separately.

Almond and Pistachio Dessert

SERVES 2

75 g/2¾ oz unsalted butter
200 g/7 oz ground almonds
200 g/7 oz sugar
150 ml/5 fl oz single cream
8 almonds, chopped
10 pistachio nuts, chopped

1. Melt the butter in a heavy-based saucepan, preferably non-stick, stirring well. Add the ground almonds, sugar and cream, stirring well. Reduce the heat and stir constantly for 10–12 minutes, scraping the base of the saucepan.

2. Increase the heat until the mixture turns a little darker in colour.

3. Transfer the almond mixture to a large, shallow serving dish and smooth the top with the back of a spoon.

4. Decorate the top of the dessert with the chopped almonds and pistachio nuts. Leave to set for 1 hour, then cut into diamond shapes and serve cold.

Salt Lassi

SERVES 4–6

700 ml/1¼ pints natural yogurt
½ tsp salt
¼ tsp sugar
250 ml/9 fl oz cold water
ice cubes
ground cumin and fresh mint sprigs, to decorate

1. Beat together the yogurt, salt and sugar in a jug or bowl, then add the water and whisk until frothy.

2. Fill 4 or 6 glasses with ice cubes and pour over the yogurt mixture. Lightly dust the top of each glass with ground cumin and decorate with mint sprigs.

Sweet Lassi

SERVES 4

500 ml/18 fl oz low-fat natural yogurt
225 ml/8 fl oz iced water
4 tbsp caster sugar
crushed ice
finely chopped pistachio nuts, to decorate

1. Pour the yogurt into a bowl and whisk with a balloon whisk or hand-held electric mixer for 1–2 minutes, or until frothy.

2. Add the water and sugar and whisk until the sugar has dissolved. Pour into a jug, cover with clingfilm and leave to chill in the refrigerator for 30 minutes.

3. Fill tall glasses with crushed ice and pour in the lassi. Sprinkle with chopped pistachios to decorate and serve immediately.

Masala Tea

SERVES 4–6

1 litre/1¾ pints water
2.5-cm/1-inch piece fresh ginger, roughly chopped
1 cinnamon stick
3 green cardamom pods, bruised
3 cloves
1½ tbsp Assam tea leaves
sugar and milk, to taste

1. Pour the water into a heavy-based saucepan over a medium–high heat. Add the ginger, cinnamon, cardamom and cloves and bring to the boil. Reduce the heat and simmer for 10 minutes.

2. Put the tea leaves in a teapot and pour over the water and spices. Stir and leave to infuse for 5 minutes.

3. Strain the tea into teacups and add sugar and milk to taste.

Ginger Cordial

SERVES 4–6

70 g/2½ oz fresh ginger, very finely chopped
½ tbsp finely grated lemon rind
1.2 litres/2 pints boiling water
2 tbsp fresh lemon juice, or to taste
4 tbsp caster sugar, or to taste
lemon slices and mint sprigs, to decorate

1. Put the ginger in a heatproof bowl with the lemon rind. Pour over the boiling water, stir and leave to steep overnight.

2. Strain the liquid into a large jug. Stir in the lemon juice and sugar, stirring until the sugar dissolves. Taste and add extra lemon juice or sugar to taste. Decorate with lemon slices and mint sprigs and serve.

Mango Cooler

SERVES 4

2 slightly underripe mangoes
1 litre/1¾ pints iced water
4 tsp sugar
crushed ice
salt
fresh mango slices, to decorate

1. Place the mangoes in a heavy-based saucepan and add just enough water to cover. Bring to the boil, then reduce the heat and simmer for 10 minutes. Drain well and leave to cool.

2. Carefully peel off the mango skins, then use a sharp knife to scrape away the flesh from the large central stones into a bowl.

3. Add the water and stir well to mix, then stir in the sugar and season with salt to taste. Stir well again, taste and add more sugar, if necessary. Fill tall glasses with crushed ice, pour in the mango cooler and decorate with mango slices. Serve immediately.

Index